the

5:2

COOKBOOK
100 RECIPES
for FASTING

ANGELA DOWDEN

hamlyn

Angela Dowden is a registered nutritionist who writes on diet and health for numerous newspapers and magazines. She was awarded the Nutrition and Health Writer/Broadcaster of the Year award in 2012.

An Hachette UK Company

www.hachette.co.uk

First published in Great Britain in 2013 by
Hamlyn a division of Octopus Publishing Group Ltd
Endeavour House,189 Shaftesbury Avenue, London WC2H 8JY
www.octopusbooks.co.uk
www.octopusbooksusa.com

This edition printed in 2013

Distributed in the US by   Distributed in Canada by
Hachette Book Group USA   Canadian Manda Group
237 Park Avenue   165 Dufferin Street
New York NY 10017 USA   Toronto, Ontario, Canada M6K 3H6

ISBN 978-1-84601-466-6

Printed and bound in the USA

10 9 8 7 6 5 4 3 2 1

Standard level kitchen spoon and cup measurements are used in all recipes.

Ovens should be preheated to the specified temperature. If using a convection oven, follow the manufacturer's instructions for adjusting the time and temperature. Broilers should also be preheated.

This book includes dishes made with nuts and nut derivatives. It is advisable for those with known allergic reactions to nuts and nut derivatives and those who may be potentially vulnerable to these allergies, such as pregnant and nursing mothers, people with weakened immune systems, the elderly, babies, and children, to avoid dishes made with nuts and nut oils.

The U.S. Department of Agriculture (USDA) advises that eggs should not be consumed raw. This book contains some dishes made with raw or lightly cooked eggs. It is prudent for more vulnerable people, such as pregnant and nursing mothers, people with weakened immune systems, the elderly, babies, and young children, to avoid uncooked or lightly cooked dishes made with eggs.

CONTENTS

The 5:2 diet

Introduction

If you've picked up this book, you may already be a convert to intermittent fasting. Alternatively, you may have heard about its benefits and are wondering whether to try it. At the other end of the scale, you may be a battle-weary diet skeptic, still holding out a small hope you'll one day find the way to shape up and feel healthier permanently. Whatever your starting point or motivation, if you have a small or large amount of weight to lose and would like to feel more comfortable in your own skin, it's for you, too.

So what is the 5:2 approach to weight loss and how does it work? There are any number of ways people practice intermittent fasting, from one day of light eating a week to no food at all for several days in a row. The 5:2 approach works well for most people because it's a pragmatic solution that steers a safe, doable, and yet effective path through these extremes.

How to use the book

The 5:2 plan allows for normal eating (including treats and meals out) for five days a week and then restricts calorie intake to 500 calories a day for women and 600 calories for men (one-quarter of the normal recommended daily intake) for the other two. For most people, it's the perfect compromise that allows for socializing, family life, and work commitments, while still introducing enough calorie control to make sure you lose weight at a healthy rate.

With its delicious and innovative recipe selection, this book shows just how flexibly you can consume your 500 or 600 calories to keep the hunger wolf at bay and, yes, even tickle your taste buds at the same time! It also includes some sweet treats, but they are perfectly suitable for a fast day, because they're not too high in sugar.

Ultimately, you'll be losing weight—as can only ever be the case—by eating, overall, fewer calories than your body uses. However, where the 5:2 diet is particularly wonderful is how marvelously achievable it can make this task for food lovers. People who find success with 5:2 often report that they failed to lose weight in the past because cutting back every day was such a struggle—doing so for just a couple of days a week, albeit more drastically, is a much more attractive proposition.

Better still, far from being a short-term fad, those who practice intermittent fasting find it is a lifestyle choice that they can stick to, because it doesn't take over their whole life, doesn't demonize specific foods, and can even run alongside other supportive weight-loss programs, such as online food diary methods.

As to the health benefits? As you lose body fat and get trimmer, you can expect to greatly reduce your chance of having a heart attack or developing heart disease.

And, in strands of research unrelated to the weight-loss benefits, there's a growing groundswell of science that shows that periodically putting your body into a fasted state may cause various chemical changes linked with lower risk of age-related diseases and higher chance of living healthier for longer.

Whether you're a 5:2 fan in search of food inspiration, or just intrigued to know more, you'll find something in this book for you. Read, digest, get slimmer, and enjoy!

IS THE 5:2 DIET FOR EVERYONE?

Most overweight adults can benefit from a 5:2 diet, but it should never be embarked on by children or adolescents, for whom any form of nutritional stress is undesirable. Also, do not do the 5:2 diet if any of the following apply (check with your medical practitioner if you are uncertain).

- You are pregnant, trying to get pregnant, or nursing.
- You are already at the bottom end of your healthy weight. You can check this using an online Body Mass Index (BMI) calculator (see page 38) —a BMI of 20 or less would indicate you are not a candidate for 5:2, or indeed any weight-loss program.
- You are an elite athlete or in training for a marathon or other big stamina event (although normal levels of activity can be undertaken on the 5:2 diet—see page 32).
- You are diabetic.
- You have irritable bowel syndrome
- You have been diagnosed with an eating disorder, either recently or in the past.

How does intermittent fasting work?

People have fasted—out of choice or through necessity—for millennia, so the general concept is far from new. Interest was roused in the 1930s (and repeatedly since), when scientists found that restricting the calories fed to various animals and insects increased their lifespan. The idea of severely restricting calories every other day—instead of by a smaller amount every day—came later, in 2003, with laboratory research carried out at the U.S. National Institute on Aging (NIA). The concept of intermittent fasting—and more specifically the 5:2 diet—for managing weight reached a mass audience when Dr. Michael Mosley presented the theories in a BBC *Horizon* television program aired in the UK in August 2012.

The IGF-1 advantage

Most people are more than happy with the tangible benefits—a flatter stomach and streamlined thighs—that intermittent fasting can bring. However, experts are interested in what it may do to our internal chemistry, in particular a hormone called IGF-1, or insulin-like growth factor. IGF-1 is important for growth when we are young but, in adulthood, lower IGF-1 levels are better, because they are linked with a less rapid turnover of cells and, potentially, a decreased cancer risk.

What's been discovered is that fasting can lower levels of IGF-1 and that a modest protein diet (as opposed to a typically meat-packed Western one) can have this effect, too. IGF-1 levels don't stay depressed for long when you return to normal eating, so the repeated on/off pattern of intermittent fasting might help keep levels persistently lower and healthier. It's a fascinating area of research with plenty still to be discovered.

Fasting is nothing new!

Fasting for physical well-being and spiritual reflection is as old as the hills and all of the big religions, such as Judaism, Buddhism, Christianity, and Islam, embrace it. It's only in modern times that we've become obsessed by the notion that we'll grow weak and depleted if we don't graze on food around the clock. In fact, you don't have to think too long about it to realize that a menu of regularly spaced meals and snacks is probably more alien to our body than periods of feast followed by periods of famine. For cavemen and women, there would undoubtedly have been periods when they were subsisting on only berries, roots, and leaves until the next animal kill, when they were able to stock up on concentrated calories ready for lean times ahead.

Nowadays, despite being bombarded with never-ending eating opportunities, our bodies are still designed with a biology and hormones that expect food to be scarce at some times and more plentiful at others. This is why many scientists believe intermittent fasting could be a particularly healthy and physiologically appropriate way to keep trim and fight aging.

As well as suiting our biology, intermittent fasting also works well on a psychological level. The "carrot" of being able to eat without depriving yourself for five days a week far outweighs the "stick" of two much tougher days each week.

Addressing 5:2 diet concerns

Any "new" eating program will probably attract critical attention, and intermittent fasting is no exception, especially given there are any number of versions with various levels of sensibleness and safety.

Suffice to say, as a registered nutritionist, I had to be completely confident that the particular version of 5:2 fasting described in these pages can do no harm. And, for the record, I am completely confident that this is so. However, to deal with some specific points that might worry you, read on.

HAVEN'T STUDIES SHOWN THAT PEOPLE FIND INTERMITTENT FASTING HARDER THAN NORMAL CALORIE COUNTING?

This worried me, too, when I read a 2011 paper by Dr. Michelle Harvie and the team at Genesis Breast Cancer Prevention, a charity in Manchester, England. It compared obese women following a 5:2-style program with obese women on modest calorie restriction every day, and it found fewer of those in the intermittent fasting group reported that they would continue with the program. Dr. Harvie has since modified and improved the diet, however, and in a further, more recent clinical trial, her subjects were significantly more likely to stick to the fasting program than normal calorie restriction. I guess this usefully illustrates the importance of finding a version of 5:2 eating that you can actually *enjoy*. However, let's not pretend that any one program is always going to work for everyone—if something doesn't work for you, don't do it!

FASTING MAY BE OKAY FOR MEN, BUT ISN'T IT BAD FOR WOMEN?
The basis of this argument seems to be that women have lower lean tissue levels and, therefore, have less reserve if skipped meals lead to the breakdown of essential muscle. Even if this were a concern—and studies of moderate intermittent fasting regimes suggest it's not—this is covered by eating modest amounts of protein on your fast day (see Fast Day Eating guidelines on page 19). Another small study that compared the experiences of eight nonobese men and women might also seem a blow to females, because it concluded that intermittent fasting seemed to "adversely affect glucose tolerance in nonobese women but not in nonobese men." However, the subjects were on a harsh program with no food at all for 36 hours in every 48-hour period. Obese women following much gentler routines, like the one advocated in this book, show very good responses in blood glucose levels and markers of diabetes risk (see page 13).

I HEARD IT COULD AFFECT FERTILITY?
As long as you eat your 500 calories on fast days, you're not being too extreme, and there is no evidence whatsoever that female fertility will be affected. Being very overweight is much more likely to affect your fertility, and 5:2 is an effective way to tackle being overweight. However, to be on the safe side, don't follow a 5:2 diet if you are actively trying for a baby. Being very thin will also affect fertility.

DOESN'T "FASTING" ENCOURAGE EATING DISORDERS?
We're being very clear that you shouldn't try intermittent fasting if you have ever had an eating disorder. This is just to be safe in case it unearths any old obsessive behaviors. More lengthy forms of fasting may be somewhat addictive, but 5:2 isn't a food-free fast at all, it's just a restricted-calorie one. There is no evidence at all that it can trigger a new eating disorder.

ISN'T SKIPPING MEALS BAD FOR YOU?
If skipping meals is part of a generally erratic and unhealthy pattern of eating, where you lurch from one unhealthy snack to another in lieu of proper balanced meals, then yes. However, with the type of controlled food restriction advocated by 5:2, the focus is on getting good nutrition despite having few calories. There's now also plenty of evidence showing that, far from being bad for you, periods with no or little food intake are actually healthy, provided, as outlined on page 7 and above, you don't have a medical or psychological condition that prohibits it.

HOW ABOUT BREAKFAST?

Skipping this meal is particularly frowned upon by experts, but most intermittent fasters will eat it on a fast day. However, don't force yourself to do so if you prefer not to; although breakfast eating is clearly associated with better health and weight, breakfast eaters also tend to have many other healthy habits, such as watching saturated fat intake and doing more exercise, which collectively explain the benefits.

ARE 5:2 ROUTINES STRICT ENOUGH TO GET MAXIMAL HEALTH BENEFITS?

One criticism, usually from academic quarters, is that 5:2 fasting doesn't actually deliver as many health benefits as it could and that periods of 18–36 hours without food are needed for potential protection against conditions such as Alzheimer's and cancer. This is at odds with what's conventionally thought safe and sensible, so is there a sensible compromise? If you want to potentially maximize the benefits of 5:2, one way *may* be to try eating just one meal on your fast day, and to make it lunch or dinner (you could try a combination of dishes from our recipe section). However, fasting in any prolonged fashion is beyond the remit of this book, and the focus of our 5:2 advice is safe and efficient weight loss, so never do anything that feels uncomfortable.

CAN IT AFFECT SLEEP AND STRESS LEVELS?

There have been some reports that fasting can lead to people sleeping more fitfully or feeling more anxious, which may be linked with changes in blood sugar level. However, such side effects are much more likely to occur with intense fasting programs than they are with the more moderate 5:2 routine. To minimize the potential for such effects, spread out your food on a fast day and choose carbohydrates with lower GIs (see page 20).

WILL I NEED VITAMIN SUPLLEMENTS?

5:2 does not advocate the cutting out of any foods or food groups, and so is less likely to leave you short of nutrients than more faddy programs. If you use 5:2 as an opportunity to overhaul your eating habits for the good, there should be even less reason to need supplements. However, some people, women in particular, can find that nutrient intakes become borderline when they cut calories. If you do choose to take a supplement, make it a basic A–Z style one.

The health benefits of intermittent fasting

As with any emerging new science, intermittent fasting attracts a variety of expert opinion and debate, from "evidence that intermittent fasting can have health benefits is very strong" (Professor Mark Mattson, Chief of the Laboratory of Neurosciences at the U.S. National Institute on Aging) to "limited evidence base for intermittent fasting in general" (from the UK's National Health Services, or NHS).

What's undeniable is that the research into the health benefits of intermittent fasting is really picking up and, although to date the number of human studies may have been small, this is rapidly changing, with new results coming out all the time.

In fact, so much so that it's hard to keep up unless you're immersed on a daily basis in this academic area—which is probably why www.nhs.uk scattered its review of 5:2 dieting with caveats warning readers it was an "unsystematic review" and "not an exhaustive 'last word' on the topic." Suffice to say, the top researchers in the area of intermittent fasting—most of them at American universities—tend to get a lot more excited and evangelical than serious academics normally have a wont to do when it comes to their particular areas of research. Many practiCe intermittent fasting themselves—and often hard-core versions—because they are so convinced of the benefits.

So what do we know are the benefits of intermittent fasting so far?

Weight loss

When you only eat 500 or 600 calories for two days a week and don't significantly overcompensate during the remaining five days (as evidence shows most people don't), it stands to reason that weight will start to drop. However, research suggests that intermittent fasting may help people remove excess weight in a more efficient and effective way than normal calorie restriction.

In particular, a 2011 review by researchers at the University of Illinois at Chicago found that people who did alternate day fasting (a repeating pattern of one day unrestricted eating followed by one day of no- or low-calorie fasting—see also page 38) were more likely to retain higher amounts of muscle tissue while losing at least as much fat. This is important because muscle helps to keep your metabolic rate higher, in essence because it is much more metabolically active than other tissues. In short, by having a more muscular frame, you can continue to burn more calories all day every day, even when you are resting, which is very helpful in managing your weight over the longer term.

What doesn't kill you makes you stronger

Research published in the *Journal of Nutritional Biochemistry* showed that feeding rats and mice only every other day improved the health and function of their brains, hearts, and other organs. Other studies have shown that mice and rats on intermittent fasts develop fewer cancers, are less prone to neurological disorders, and live 30 percent longer than their siblings that were fed every day. All this is fascinating stuff that's driving the new wave of human studies, but what's particularly interesting is that experts think it's the *stress* that fasting puts on the body that does the good!

According to Professor Mark Mattson—the world's most cited neuroscientist as reported in *New Scientist* magazine—fasting is a type of hormesis, a process whereby organisms exposed to low levels of stress or toxins become more resistant to tougher challenges. For example, the mild biological stress induced by fasting causes cells in the heart and digestive system to produce proteins that decrease heart rate and blood pressure and increase digestion motility (the movement of food through the digestive system), reducing the risk of heart disease, stroke, and colon cancer. It really does seem to be a case of what doesn't kill you (i.e., managing on minimum food for a couple of days a week) makes you stronger!

Diabetes and blood sugar control

Any amount of weight loss in obese individuals, however it is achieved, will generally result in the body becoming more sensitive to insulin, which is an important step toward reducing the risk of diabetes (exercise has the effect of making you more responsive to insulin, too). However, intermittent fasting could have a particularly good effect on your blood sugar control and diabetes risk.

In one of Dr. Michelle Harvie's studies for Genesis Breast Cancer Prevention at Manchester's Wyntheshawe Hospital, women who were on a 5:2-style intermittent fasting diet (largely milk and vegetables, adding up to 650 calories for two days each week, and a Mediterranean-style diet for the rest of the time), were compared with women who were restricted to 1,500 calories every day.

In both groups, women lost weight, reduced their cholesterol levels, recorded lower blood pressures, and had reduced markers of breast cancer risk. When it came to reductions in fasting insulin and insulin resistance—both signs that diabetes risk has decreased—the benefits, though modest, were greater in the 5:2 diet group than those using conventional calorie restriction.

Heart disease

As I have alluded, a reduction in cardiovascular risk factors— for example, LDL cholesterol (that's the "bad" type that carries cholesterol toward arteries, where it collects and causes "furring") and high blood pressure—can be expected on the 5:2 diet. Triglycerides in the blood will also tend to fall as you lose weight (put simply, this means that your blood is less sticky and, therefore, less liable to clot).

Much of the work in this area has been done by Dr. Krista Varady and her team at the University of Illinois at Chicago, with one of her scientific papers on the subject being entitled "Intermittent fasting combined with calorie restriction is effective for weight loss and cardio-protection in obese women" (November 2012). The research outlines the benefit that intermittent fasting, and wider, healthy weight loss, can contribute to a healthy heart. The results are made clear in the paper's title.

Brain function

Much of the research into intermittent fasting actually started, and continues, in the healthy aging field, and brain aging in particular. At the U.S. National Institute on Aging, they've been investigating rats and mice that have been genetically engineered to develop Alzheimer's disease. Given normal circumstances, these animals show obvious signs of dementia by the time they are a year old (getting disorientated in a maze that they have previously been able to navigate with ease, for example), but when they're put on an on/off fasting program, they don't develop dementia until they're around 20 months, or much nearer the natural end of their lives.

What could be the reason? One thing that's been reported is that the fasting mouse brain produces more of a protein called BDNF (brain-derived neurotrophic factor), which stimulates the growth of new nerve cells in the hippocampus part of the brain, essential for learning and memory. There's certainly an evolutionary logic for the fasting state to be linked with better cognitive function, too. If you were hungry in caveman days, you needed your wits about you to track down the next meal and survive.

As yet, there are still many unknowns (for example, whether longer periods of fasting are needed than normally experienced on a 5:2 diet) and the human studies have still to be done, so it's impossible to say if intermittent fasting will help to prevent dementia. However, it's certainly an interesting area of research, and one to watch.

Cancer

Much of the published research into the potential disease-protective effects of intermittent fasting involve measuring a biological marker named insulin-like growth factor-1 (IGF-1), which is known to be associated with cancer. Fasting has the effect of reducing IGF-1 levels, at least temporarily, and also seems to stimulate genes that repair our cells.

However, how a reduction in IGF-1 translates into successful real-world outcomes (i.e., a reduced chance of people getting cancer) is still unclear. One 2007 clinical review did look at "real-world" health outcomes and concluded that intermittent fasting (specifically, alternate day fasting, which usually has minimum 18-hour periods without food) may have a protective effect against cancer, as well as heart disease and diabetes. However, it concluded "research is required to establish definitively the consequences," which is a fair reflection of the science as it currently is. In short, how effective intermittent fasting is against cancer relative to other healthy-eating or weight-loss routines is still to be clarified.

COULD 5:2 MAKE YOU HAPPIER?

Anecdotally, many 5:2 eaters say their low-calorie intake makes them feel more clear-headed, more able to concentrate, and even more cheerful. It's uncertain as to why this should be, but feeling more upbeat will certainly make it easier to refuse that slice of cake.

Getting started

The beauty of the 5:2 diet is that, beyond the requirement for two 500- or 600-calorie days a week, there are no firm rules and it's flexible. As with all new healthy habits, however, it can take time to adjust and the hunger aspect can initially be hard. On the plus side, the results you begin to see and feel within a short period of time will make your fast days quickly become less of a chore, and even something you can begin to enjoy. Preparation and planning are key.

Choose your fasting days

As a first step, you'll need to decide which days will work best for you as fasting days. This may evolve over time, or from week to week, according to your circumstances. As a general rule, you're more likely to stick to the routine if you can repeat the same two days every week, so try to choose days that you'll need to deviate from only infrequently. For example, don't pick a Tuesday if this is the day when a friend is most likely to invite you around for lunch, or a Friday if you're going to be tempted by a takeout after work. For obvious reasons, weekend days may not be such good fasting days either, but everyone's different and you should choose what works for you.

Whether you run the two days consecutively or apart is also up to you, and there isn't enough research to say definitively that one way or another is best. Most people doing 5:2 for themselves, rather than in the context of a highly monitored clinical trial, simply find it easiest in terms of managing hunger and keeping on track to have a gap between fasting days. However, if two days together suits you better, and you feel energetic and motivated, there's no reason why you shouldn't do it this way.

THE GENDER DIVIDE

On a fasting day:

- If you're a man, you should have no more than 600 calories.
- If you're a woman, you should have no more than 500 calories.
- It is a fact that, even if a man and a woman weigh the same, the man will usually have a higher metabolism than the woman, because he has a higher proportion of muscle (see page 10).

Fast day meals

The second decision to make is how you will spread your 500 or 600 calories over the fasting day. Again, this is down to personal preference, usually honed through trial and error. A satisfying format for many people is to bookend their day with two meals—a 100–200-calorie breakfast and a 300-calorie dinner, for example, with the possibility of 100 calories or so for snacking or another small meal in between, if desired. Other people report they are happier if they don't eat their first morsel until brunch or lunch, while still others (usually men, on anecdotal evidence) prefer saving up their calories for just one reasonable-size meal—either a lunch or an evening meal.

One argument for leaving your first calorie intake until lunch or later is that the stretch of time you go without food is longer—perhaps 18 hours or more—which some researchers have surmised may be associated with potentially bigger health benefits (see page 11). (By comparison, the longest you'd go without food if you eat breakfast on your fasting day will probably be around 12 hours.)

However, many people, perhaps women in particular, prefer to graze their way through fast days, and Dr. Michelle Harvie's research offers some reassurance here. It found that obese women eating three small, evenly spaced mini meals on two nonconsecutive fasting days per week lost weight efficiently and also reduced inflammatory chemicals that increase breast cancer risk.

The main point is to find what suits you and not to shoehorn yourself into a routine that doesn't fit your lifestyle. We simply don't know the optimum food-free stretch, if there is any optimum at all.

To find a pattern of food intake that enables you to stick to your 5:2 plans and achieve sustainable weight loss, try keeping a food and mood diary. Making a note of how you feel physically and mentally on fast days can be an effective way to track how well you're coping with the program. Simply write down what foods/meals you eat, when you have them, and any accompanying feelings of hunger, mood, or wavering willpower. Registering when you feel at your weakest and strongest on a fast day can help you to tailor future fast days so that they are easier.

More than 500 or 600 calories?

Some programs allow up to 700 calories on fast days, but if you increase calories on these two days, you'll probably have to look at introducing some restrictions on the other five days, too. The amount of 500 or 600 calories is 25 percent of the normal average calorie requirement, and emulates the protocol used by some preliminary but successful alternate day fasting human studies completed at the University of Illinois at Chicago (a 5:2 fasting program is a more achievable version of alternate day fasting, and you'll probably find it easier to stick to).

While a handful of calories either way isn't going to make much difference, if it becomes obvious you're going to breach 500 or 600 calories by a large amount, abandon ship, and count the day as a nonfast one.

WHAT DOES 500 CALORIES LOOK LIKE?

Admittedly not a lot—but then that is, after all, somewhat the point. As a rough guide, 500 calories would be:

- Breakfast: ¾ cup (1 ounce) of bran flakes with ½ cup low-fat milk, plus ½ cup (3 ounces) each of blueberries and strawberries (200 calories).
- Dinner: 1 ¾ cups (6½ ounces) of canned bean soup followed by 3½ ounces shrimp with a dessert bowl of salad of arugula, bell peppers, tomato, and cucumber dressed with 1 tablespoon of low-fat balsamic dressing 250 calories).
- Snack: ½ banana (50 calories).
- Men have another 100 calories to play with, which is the equivalent of adding half a slice of toast spread with 2 teaspoons of peanut butter.

If this looks daunting, don't worry—there are a lot of tips for making your fasting day as painless as possible in the following pages. While most intermittent fasters will find it challenging at first, the process gets much easier as your body adapts.

Fast day eating

Theoretically, you could have a large burger and endless cups of black coffee on a fast day and be within your calorie allowance, but clearly this wouldn't be good for you. Instead, it's a great idea to use your fasting day to make balanced and healthy choices, using the following guidelines.

Eat five a day

Your fast day is the perfect opportunity to fill up on fruit and vegetables because these foods are bulky and low in calories, take up plenty of room on your plate (a psychological boost), and are linked with a lower risk of killer diseases, such as heart disease and cancer. Green leafy vegetables, such as spinach, kale, watercress, arugula, broccoli, and cabbage, are particularly low in calories, as are berries, such as strawberries and raspberries, which you'll often find in convenient form in the freezer section of the supermarket. Tomatoes, bell peppers, orange-fleshed melons, and butternut squash join the low-calorie corner—the wonderful thing about all these richly colored fruit and vegetables is they consistently appear in superfood lists because of their high antioxidant content (antioxidants are the component in fruit and vegetables that mop up the free radicals that can damage our cells).

In short, by using your fast day as a chance to eat at least five colorful portions of fruit and vegetables a day (a portion is around 3 ounces, or roughly a handful), you'll be boosting your health as well as benefiting your waistline.

Dairy and beans

These two deserve a special mention because they're unusual in providing a combination of carbohydrates and protein in one easy package and are a great source of vitamins and minerals. They can be easy on the waistline, too—notfat Greek yogurt (a great topping for fruit) has only 57 calories in a 3½-ounce serving of about ½ cup, while creamy canned lima beans (fabulous to bulk out a salad) have 56 calories in a 2½-ounce serving of about ⅓ cup.

Include lean protein

The lowest calorie lean protein sources (all weighing in at less than 100 calories for a 3½-ounce portion) include shrimp, tofu, and tuna canned in water, though grilled fish, eggs, and chicken breast are also good choices. Including one or more of these protein foods on a fast day is to be recommended, because you're be more likely to preserve valuable muscle tissue during periods of calorie restriction when protein is consumed (and particularly if you exercise, too). Another big bonus is that protein is particularly good at keeping you full, so can help to keep hunger pangs at bay for longer. Digesting it also uses up more calories than does digesting other nutrients, which is all grist to the mill of your diminishing middle!

Choose good-quality carbs

Admittedly you won't be able to eat very big carbohydrate portions on a fast day (there are around 100 calories in just one slice of bread, for example), but it's a good idea to make sure any modest portions you do choose are as unprocessed or nutrient rich as possible, and to focus on higher fiber choice where you can. Whole-wheat breads, rolled oats, whole-wheat pasta, pearl barley, fortified whole-grain breakfast cereals, and potatoes in their skins tend to have a relatively low glycemic index, or GI, which means they raise blood sugar levels only relatively slowly, helping to keep blood sugar, energy, and appetite levels more controlled.

Perhaps more important, however, is *not* to spend too many (if any) of your fast day calories on sweet and sugary carbohydrates, such as cookies or dessert. (A rough rule of thumb would be for women to use no more than 50 calories on these foods, and men no more than 100 calories.) Quite apart from their lack of nutrient value, they'll really challenge your ability to stay on track, because they can cause your blood sugar levels to fluctuate, heightening feelings of hunger.

PERFECT FAST DAY PROPORTIONS

- Concentrate on fruit and veg (steamed, grilled, stir-fried, or in soups and salads) as your main stomach-filling priority (up to 200 calories).
- Use most of the remaining calories (300 or 400) on low GI carbohydrate-rich and/or protein-rich foods.
- Any calories you have left over you can use as you like (see the lists of up to 50-calorie and 100-calorie snack suggestions on pages 44–46). But choosing more nutritious foods is always best.

Beverage options

It is important to stay well-hydrated on fast days (see page 33), but with the exception of low-fat milk (or a milk alternative, such as soy milk), many drinks can be a wasteful, nonfilling way to spend calories. Your best options on a fast day are calorie-free drinks, such as black coffee and tea (though try not to drink more caffeine than you would normally), herbal teas, diet drinks, and, of course (and best of all), good old water. To jazz it up, try a sparkling variety and add a squeeze of lime or lemon.

Alcohol is one of the least sensible choices of all (even the smallest glass of wine has around 100 calories and could stimulate your appetite), so use your fast days to abstain from alcohol altogether and give your liver two days a week of important rest.

TOP TIPS FOR BEGINNERS

- The day before your first fast, eat well and aim to go to bed feeling neither hungry nor overfull. Getting an early night is good preparation. Trying to stuff in as much food as late as possible so you don't feel hungry tomorrow is not.

- Do your eating homework so that you know how you are going to spend your 500 or 600 calories, and which meals you are going to spread them between. Use the recipes in this book as inspiration and make sure you are stocked up with the requisite ingredients.

- Make your environment as devoid of food temptations as possible, which means being sure a stray slice of cold pizza isn't the thing screaming "eat me!" when you open the refrigerator.

- Arm yourself with some kind of calorie counter—there is one to get you started on pages 152–57—or you can use an online app or Web site.

- Be aware that choosing a less busy day to start your fasting may not be the best approach. As long as you have your food choices preplanned, a day with plenty to keep you occupied may be better.

- If you find your first fast too hard and have to give in, you've probably just chosen the wrong day. Don't despair and try again another time, but wait a few days.

Fast day feel-full tips

• Water is the perfect slimline filler, either drunk on its own to temporarily take the edge off a hunger pang or, more particularly, incorporated within food to increase satiety (the feeling of fullness that food imparts). Chunky soups plus a lot of fruit and vegetables can work particularly well on a fast day, because they'll help to make your stomach feel full.

• Airy foods take up more space on your plate (so, psychologically, it feels like you're being presented with more food), as well as in your stomach. One study by Professor Barbara Rolls at Pennsylvania State University, published in the journal *Appetite*, compared the same snack in a puffed and nonpuffed version and found that those receiving the airy snack ate 73 percent more in volume, but consumed 21 percent fewer calories. Rice cakes are the ultimate airy food, and a whipped mousse (which can have fewer than 80 calories per serving) is the way to go if you really can't do without dessert!

• Protein-rich foods are particularly good at inducing satiety. One theory is that they stimulate the release of hunger-controlling hormones in the digestive tract. The protein in eggs seems particularly good at keeping you full.

• Whole-grain versions of breakfast cereals, breads, pasta, rice, and noodles take longer to chew and are more satisfying, because the fiber they contain provides bulk but no calories. Fiber also has a slowing effect on the passage of food through the digestive tract, which has the effect of keeping you fuller for longer. The portion size of bread or pasta you can have on a fast day is small, but choosing a whole-grain, not white, version can help to make it more filling.

• Focus on whole foods. On average, foods that aren't highly processed, packaged, or high in sugar will tend to be lower GI and keep your blood sugar levels on a more even keel.

Don't estimate!

Building up an accurate picture of what actually constitutes 500 or 600 calories (see the box on page 18) is one of the most educational and interesting aspects of the 5:2 diet. It can help you understand what constitutes a healthy portion and might also give a clue to why you ended up needing to lose a few pounds in the first place.

It won't come as a surprise, then, that "estimates" and "educated guesses" are definitely not okay when it comes to calculating your fast day calories. With the best will in the world, you'll almost certainly be wrong, which will jeopardize your weight loss and dilute the health benefits. If you're not convinced, try seeing if you can correctly estimate the "recommended" 1-ounce serving of flake-style breakfast cereal, such as ¾ cup of bran flakes. Most people pour nearer to 1¼ to 1½ cups into the bowl, which can add more than 100 "accidental" calories and completely destroy a fasting day.

It's also important to measure the ingredients carefully when you're making the recipes in this book, so they don't exceed the calorie counts given. If you don't own standard measuring cups and spoons, you need to lay your hands on them. A small investment in an electronic kitchen scale, available in the kitchen section of larger department stores and on the Internet, will be helpful in determining the correct portions.

At first, you should weigh everything until you've got a clearer idea of what different-size portions weigh. Your idea of a "medium" apple—3½ ounces with peel but no core, according to some official publications—may be very different to mine or someone else's.

If it seems like a pain, it's really not—it's actually fun learning about calories and portion sizes and, as you're only doing it two days a week and you're not eating that much on those days either, it shouldn't be too onerous. Look at it as a chance to really understand what you are putting into your mouth.

WHAT ABOUT SWEETENERS?

Sugar substitutes, including aspartame, sucralose, and more recently stevia, have been approved by health authorities around the world, yet there still seems to be a host of scare stories circulating about how they could actually make us fatter or even cause cancer. In the end, it's up to you if you want to use them or not, but if adding a little sweetness to a bowl of berries or to a cup of tea makes you more inclined to stay on track with your 5:2 diet, then go ahead and use them. Unless you're eating sweeteners in vast quantities, they are unlikely to do any harm and are a much better bet on fast day than spoonfuls of sugar.

"Off" day eating

Of necessity, some time has been spent explaining about fasting days, what to eat on them and how to make sure they're successful. But let's not forget that the beauty of 5:2, and the core reason that it appeals to, and works for, so many people, is that you can have five days each week without worrying about cutting a single calorie!

Does that mean you can truly eat anything you want to? Well, yes, but naturally there are limits. The good news? Studies consistently show that contrary to what you might expect, intermittent fasters are actually unlikely to go on a big binge on their "off" days. Instead of making your appetite more extreme, 5:2 dieting seems to help naturally regulate it so you enjoy only as much food as you need when you aren't fasting. However, if your journey to 5:2 eating has involved a lifetime of flip-flopping between failed diets and bingeing, it may take longer for a healthy relationship with food to develop.

Am I hungry, am I full?

While 5:2 fasting can ultimately help you regulate your food intake and weight without micromanaging every mouthful, the thought of genuinely being able to eat what you want for five days a week may seem a little scary at first. If so, you may need a little hand-holding until you can get to a point where you trust your eating intuition.

One simple technique that can help is to regularly rate your hunger on a scale of 1 to 10 throughout the day. On this scale, 1 is ravenously, stomach growlingly hungry, whereas 10 is completely stuffed to the point of discomfort. As the ideal is for you to feel reasonably hungry before a meal and comfortably satisfied afterward, the aim is not to start eating until you register 4 or below on the scale, and to stop putting food in your mouth when you hit 7 or 8.

Chewing thoroughly before swallowing, putting your knife and fork down between bites, and taking at least 20 minutes over a meal are all other great tips to help you slow down, notice, and appreciate what you are eating and naturally self-regulate your food intake.

Is it head hunger?

Over time, your fast days will help teach you what it's like to feel physically hungry, so you can distinguish between when you need to eat and when you only have an urge to do so. Here are a few ways you can distinguish between head hunger (fake) and stomach hunger (real).

HEAD HUNGER
• Is something you probably experience in association with negative emotions, such as frustration or anger, or as a response to stress, boredom, or habit.
• Is nonhungry eating, stimulated by the likes of food ads on TV.
• Will be experienced as something like a nagging voice in your head, convincing you that you're having a bad day so it's fine to eat.

STOMACH HUNGER
• Is a physical sensation—your stomach rumbles and feels empty.
• Is still there and stronger 20 minutes after you distract yourself with a nonfood-related activity.
• Only usually happens three or so hours after your last proper meal, dependent on what you ate.

Balanced eating

If you do feel like you need the security of calorie counting on "off" days, the best advice is to stick to around 1,900–2,000 calories if you are a woman and around 2,400–2,500 if you are a man. This would be the average "weight maintenance" level of calories if you were entering your food intake into a weight-loss Web site.

"Off" days have plenty of scope to include treats (see box below), but nonfast days should include a good balance of wholesome foods, too. As a guideline, ideally the following food groups should be included daily to be sure you get the nutrients your body requires. This is not a lecture about foods you *must* eat—just some helpful hints, should you need them, on how to eat well.

WHAT DOES 2,000 CALORIES LOOK LIKE?

As a guide, 2,000 calories might look something like this:

• Breakfast: Poached egg, two cooked bacon strips, broiled tomato and mushrooms, small glass of orange juice.
• Lunch: Chicken salad sandwich, container of fruit yogurt, grapes and melon slices.
• Dinner: Chili con carne, broccoli and carrots, small serving of apple crisp.
• Snacks: Package of chips, thin chocolate-coated cookie bar.

FRUIT AND VEGETABLES

As with your fast days, try to include five different portions of fruit and vegetables daily for their fiber, vitamin, mineral, and antioxidant content. As a rough guide, a portion is approximately the amount you can hold in your hand. All types (excluding potatoes), count, including fresh, frozen, canned, dried, and juiced.

CARBOHYDRATES

As with fast days, minimally processed, whole-grain or high-fiber types (for example, whole-wheat bread) are best, but this doesn't mean you can't also have white bread, oven fries, or naan occasionally, if you desire. At the average meal, these starchy carbohydrate foods should ideally take up around one-quarter of the space on your plate to help provide the energy, B vitamins, and fiber your body needs.

PROTEIN

At an ideal meal, protein would take up another quarter of your plate, about the same size as the carb serving. Protein is needed for muscles

CAN I EAT A HIGH-FAT DIET AND STILL LOSE WEIGHT?

As it happens, you can. In a fascinating study published in the January 2013 edition of the journal *Metabolism—Clinical and Experimental*, alternate day intermittent fasters lost similar amounts of weight, including from around their waist, whether they got a whopping 45 percent of their calories from fat, or a more abstemious 25 percent. Both groups also showed reductions in cardiovascular risk factors, including blood levels of cholesterol and triglycerides. Of important note, though, is that subjects in the trial did not eat more calories on the high-fat routine.

And while people who have been used to high-fat diets may be able to stick to intermittent fasting better if they continue with the fatty foods they love, the authors say it's not such a good idea for your heart health long term. However, a moderate-fat diet of up to 35 percent of calories from fat is fine. So much the better if you swap some of those fats from the saturated to the unsaturated kind—so less butter, cream, and processed meat products, and more nuts, seeds, vegetable oils, avocados, and oily fish.

and tissues to grow or repair themselves, and it's also wonderfully satiating. On your "off" days you can focus less on choosing proteins simply according to their calorie content and leanness, and this affords greater opportunity for choosing more eco-friendly, sustainable sources. These tend to be the plant proteins—for example, beans, nuts, tofu, and textured vegetable protein products.

DAIRY OR ALTERNATIVES
Including dairy foods or fortified alternatives, such as soya, rice, oat, almond, or hazelnut milks, makes it easier to make sure you get enough calcium in your diet. In turn, this helps to keep bones strong. There's some evidence that people with dairy- or calcium-rich diets find it easier to manage their weight, too—another good reason to regularly include these foods.

Watch those portions!
An important aspect of 5:2 is that you don't have to feel bound by any eating rules on your "off" days. However, supersize portions are worth a special mention because they are so prevalent and can really distort our perception of what is an appropriate amount to eat.

COFFEE
Once, a standard serving was perhaps an 8 fluid-ounce cup of instant coffee (about 45 calories with milk and sugar). Now, the smallest size in coffee shops is at least 12 fluid ounces, or 1½ cups, and it's not unusual to see coffee sizes up to 2½ cups. Opt for a medium mocha coffee with low-fat milk and whipped cream, and you'll be downing 315 calories—more than a McDonald's cheeseburger!

To beat portion distortion, go for basic filter coffee, or at most a skinny latte (102 calories for a 12-fluid-ounce size).

HOME-COOKED DISHES
Analysis of recipes in the 2006 edition of one of America's favorite cookbooks, *Joy of Cooking,* found the suggested serving size of identical main courses had increased by as much as 42 percent from recipes in the first edition in 1931. The effect on dishes such as spaghetti with a meat sauce has been to add about 150 calories.

To beat portion distortion, serve on smaller plates. Moving from a 12-inch to a 10-inch dinner plate leads people to serve and eat around 22 percent less.

WINE

Most wine glasses used to contain 4 fluid ounces, or ½ cup—about 85 calories and 1.5 alcohol units—but now a "small" glass at a bar or restaurant can be 6 fluid ounces, or ¾ cup—about 120 calories. Some large glasses hold 8 fluid ounces, or a third of a bottle.

To beat portion distortion, use smaller glasses at home and buy lower alcohol wines of 12 percent or less. At the bar, stick to one glass.

PREPARED MEALS

Even our cousins across the pond are increasing their portions. A Food Standards Agency-commissioned report found prepared meals had significantly increased in size. For example, an individual beef lasagne meal morphed from 8 ounces in 1990 to 11–16 ounces in 2008.

To beat portion distortion, check the calories on the nutrition labels, which will list the size of a single serving by cup or piece, followed by weight in grams. Calories are more important than size when it comes to prepared meals. Less than 150 calories per 100 grams per serving is a reasonable level to aim for on nonfasting days.

POPCORN

According to America's National Heart, Lung, and Blood Institute (NHLBI), the average movie theater popcorn serving increased from 270 calories 20 years ago to 630 calories today. Even though you could leave those extra 360 calories behind, you probably won't.

To beat portion distortion, always opt for the smallest bucket size, even if it doesn't seem good value for money.

FAST FOOD

The NHLBI also says that an average pizza serving has 850 calories today, compared with 500 calories two decades ago. Burgers are also bigger—when McDonald's first began in 1955, its only hamburger patty weighed around 1¾ ounces. Now, it's not uncommon to have two quarter pounders (8 ounces) in one bun, and a Big Mac (490 calories) is actually on the small side compared with many burgers!

To beat portion distortion, choose a burger that's no bigger than your balled fist, and opt for small fries. Share those extra slices of pizza, or have it as leftovers on another "off" day.

What to expect on the 5:2 diet

If you have a BMI of 25 or more (to check your BMI, see page 38) when you start your 5:2 eating plan, you can expect to lose weight at an average rate of 1 pound a week until you stabilize at a healthy weight within the 18.5–25 BMI range. However, as with any form of calorie restriction, the amount you lose will vary from week to week, so expect highs, lows, and plateaus along the way. In the beginning, you may lose weight quickly—2–3 pounds isn't unusual in the first week—which can be immensely motivating. The flipside is that you risk becoming despondent in the weeks that follow if your weight loss fluctuates or slows down. The key to success is always to have the bigger picture in mind—there may be disappointments along the way, but all the evidence suggests that, in the longer term, you will succeed. While the path may not be entirely smooth, no other weight-loss program can boast that you can eat normally for five days a week and still be 14 pounds lighter in three to four months.

Measuring your progress

Before you begin the 5:2 diet, it's a good idea to know what your starting point is so you can measure your progress along the way. Some people say they prefer not to use a scale and are happy just to measure their progress in terms of a looser waistband, but this can often be about denial. No one is forcing you to weigh and measure, but if your weight has been creeping ever upward and you haven't been tracking it, it is probably best to bite the bullet, get on that scale, and face up to what your starting point may be.

MONITORING YOUR WEIGHT

Research findings from America's National Weight Control Registry—a database of people who have maintained a weight loss of 30 pounds or more for at least one year or more—show that 75 percent of weight watchers use regular weighing as part of their success strategy, and most diet and health professionals now believe that weekly monitoring of weight is a marker of diet success.

Some bathrooms scales will also give you a readout of your percentage body fat, which should show a pleasing downward trend as the weeks go by. Do be aware that different scales can give different body fat readings, however, and even the same scale will register ups and downs from one day to the next, depending on factors, such as time of day and how much fluid you've consumed. As with your weight, it's the trend over time that matters, so don't get hung up over individual measurements.

WAIST MEASUREMENT

Another simple but effective way to measure your progress is with a tape measure around your middle. Measure at the place where your waist is naturally narrowest or, if this is hard to define, at the midpoint between the top of your hip bone and the bottom of your ribs. This measurement is a reasonable proxy for the amount of internal fat you have in the central region and, in turn, a good marker for heart disease, high blood pressure, and diabetes risk. As your waist measurement falls, your risk of developing any of these conditions is steadily reduced.

For men, risk moves from high to medium as waist measurement falls below 40 inches and to low risk when the measurement goes below 37 inches. For women, the respective figures are 34½ inches and 31½ inches. People of Asian backgrounds tend to have a higher proportion of body fat to muscle and need to achieve smaller waist measurements than those of Caucasian backgrounds to achieve the same level of risk reduction.

AVAILABLE TESTS

As you progress with 5:2 fasting and the weight continues to drop off, you can also expect your level of LDL cholesterol (see page 14) to decrease, your blood pressure to come down, and your blood glucose level to shift downward. Other biomarkers—for example, those that predict cancer risk (see page 15)—will also probably improve.

Overstretched medical practitioners tend not to be best pleased when "worried well" patients demand repeated tests for no good medical reason. And less run-of-the-mill blood tests—for example, for IGF-1,

EXPECT FOOD TO TASTE WONDERFUL!

One thing that 5:2 eaters consistently report is how delicious even simple flavors taste on fast day. When you're not constantly eating, the delayed gratification that's associated with being properly hungry makes you really appreciate your food. Fresh vegetables, lean meat, and subtle natural flavors really come into their own. Because you know your meals are limited, your taste buds seem heightened and you will savor every bite, taking time over each morsel. People who had previously always shunned vegetables often start eating piles of them with 5:2, which can only be a good thing!

which has been tracked in some intermittent fasting trials— aren't covered by some medical insurance policies. However, your health-care practitioner may be willing to do simple but important check ups on your blood pressure and cholesterol level, both now and after you've lost about 14 pounds or so. If not, some pharmacies offer a fully validated cholesterol check, which is relatively inexpensive.

Dealing with hunger

At first, those gripy hunger pangs can seem insistent on fast days. However, the good news is that those feelings definitely become much less intense, with most long-term 5:2 devotees stating that they are no longer unduly troubled by fast day hunger after a few weeks. Another possibility is that intermittent fasters simply learn to embrace the feeling and not to be fazed by it.

Getting on top of initial hunger pangs can be as simple as actually experiencing those feelings and realizing that you can come out the other side without collapsing in a pile on the floor or dying of starvation. We're so programmed to eat at the slightest twinge of hunger that feeling anything more than slightly peckish can actually be alien and even a little bit scary. In time, when you realize nothing dreadful is going to happen if you feel hungry for a day, this will change and you can actually learn to appreciate the physical sensations of hunger you get on a fast day, knowing that you are in tune with your body and have tackled the art of being able to savor food without overloading your system.

However, if you're struggling in the early stages, here are some tips for riding out hunger pangs:

- Be aware that the pangs often come in waves—although you may be particularly hungry now, you probably won't be in 20 minutes if you focus on something else.
- Write a list of simple activities that will distract you from thoughts of hunger (anything from phoning a friend to cleaning your shoes). Pin it to the refrigerator as a reminder for when you start to weaken.
- Go for a run or walk, whichever suits you. It's one of the best ways to temporarily distract yourself from hunger.
- Brushing your teeth right after your evening meal on a fast day makes it less likely that you'll succumb to evening munchies. Best of all, get an early night, because you can't eat when you are asleep.

Exercise and 5:2

An exercise program can definitely complement your 5:2 weight-loss progress, and will provide many attendant health benefits, such as stronger bones and a healthier heart.

However, how should you negotiate exercise on a fast day? The old wisdom was that you should be well-fueled prior to exercise, but the latest evidence suggests that modest activity in the fasted state is actually good for you. In particular, exercising in the fasted state means that the body has to use fat as its primary fuel, which is good news for the disappearance of those love handles. Another benefit of exercising on an empty stomach appears to be that you'll build muscle better when you do get around to eating in the postexercise period.

In a nutshell, there's no reason you shouldn't work out on your fast day, with the ideal being to exercise when you are feeling hungry, perhaps in the afternoon, and then to follow with one of your fast day meals.

However, common sense must come into play, and if you're new to exercise, it's probably best to ease yourself into physical activity on only nonfast days. There's also some suggestion that women are better doing weights on fasting days (while men can particularly benefit from cardio work). Listening to your body is essential, and you should always stop exercising immediately if you feel faint, dizzy, or light-headed.

HOW ACTIVE SHOULD I BE?

Official guidelines suggest that for optimum health benefits, you should be physically active (at the level of brisk walking or gentle cycling, for example) for at least 30 minutes five times a week. If you're doing something more vigorous, such as running or playing a racquet sport, you can get away with 75 minutes, or three 25-minute sessions a week. On top of this, one or two 20-minute sessions with weights are also recommended to maintain muscle tone and lean tissue levels, particularly in the over 40s.

10 ways to make the 5:2 diet work for you

1. Be flexible

The 5:2 program is definitely not a prescriptive diet with a big list of "dos" and "don'ts" that you may have been used to in the past. That's a plus point, but it can also be a little off-putting at first if you're used to being told exactly what to do as part of a weight-loss routine.

The secret to finding the right version for you is to be prepared to road test different fasting day routines until you find the one that works best. When it comes down to it, the chance to change fasting days around is the key attraction of 5:2, and you should feel free to exploit that flexibility to it's fullest.

2. Keep well-hydrated

Fluid is your friend on fast days because it helps to give a sensation of stomach fullness, at least temporarily. Because it's also possible to confuse hunger with thirst, keeping up your intake of fluids at all times will prevent you from falling foul of this potentially waist-widening mix-up. As a bonus, water is needed for every chemical reaction in the body, including burning fat.

Don't think you must stick to plain water if you don't want to;- black tea and coffee, herbal tea, and calorie-free beverages all count toward your fluid intake, too.

3. Find a fasting buddy

Research shows that when you're tackling your weight, you'll do better if you have someone doing it alongside you. For example, a study at the University of Pennsylvania found that 66 percent of the people dieting with friends had maintained their weight loss after 10 months, compared to only 24 percent of those who were on their own.

There's no particular reason that you'll need more support with 5:2 than any other weight-loss program, and, in fact, many people do it successfully all by themselves because the periods of food deprivation are short and manageable. However, if a partner or friend wants to follow the program with you, you should jump at the chance for the extra support it brings.

4. Keep out of temptation's way

Fasting days are surprisingly doable, and with a positive mindset and some forward menu planning, you can even sit down for an evening meal (albeit with a different mix of foods on your plate) with the rest of the family. But—and it's a big and fairly logical but—there's simply no point putting yourself in temptation's way if you can avoid it!

Research at Cornell University's Food and Brand Lab in New York has identified visibility and convenience as the two biggest drivers of mindless eating, with "out of sight" being a key strategy to successful calorie control. So taking steps as simple as keeping cookies in an opaque container or in a drawer, or moving a bowl of candies from your office desk to a filing cabinet at a distance away can markedly increase your chances of staying on track on a fast day.

However, if you are faced with a food temptation, psychologists believe tightening muscles is so closely tied to determination that simply doing it can muster up greater willpower to resist. In studies, subjects were more likely to think they could resist chocolate cake while flexing their biceps, while others were better able to resist unhealthy foods at a snack bar while holding a pen woven through spread fingers (thus engaging their hand muscles). It's not hard to imagine how clenching helps, and balling your fists is certainly worth a try when faced with a strong temptation to break your fast.

5. Save chocolate for "off" days

Apart from the fact that you'll only be able to have a disappointingly teeny amount, one small study has suggested that eating chocolate when we are hungry may heighten our general desire for it. Conversely, eating it when we are full may "train" us out of a craving. Researchers at University College London split students into two groups, giving both groups half a bar of chocolate twice a day. After two weeks, the half that had been told to eat their chocolate rations on an empty stomach reported a stronger craving than before. By contrast, the students who had been eating the chocolate on a full stomach craved chocolate less and even reported that it now seemed somewhat less pleasant to the taste.

6. Consider Internet food shopping

Patrolling the aisles with your shopping cart can give you a small amount of exercise, but you may find that it's better to do Internet shopping and go for a run instead! The reason? When you're shopping for fast day food, supermarkets can be a toxic environment in the sense that the sights, smells, and deli counters can lure you to put things in your basket that you hadn't got on your list and didn't intend to buy. On your five "off" days, you can, of course, choose whatever foods you want, but many people do find they start to develop a natural inclination to eat a more balanced and healthy diet overall, which Internet shopping is potentially more supportive of. Certainly, if your grocery shopping starts to involve a lot of label reading (often in a challenging small print), it may be easier to do this food-sleuthing at the click of a mouse instead of in the store itself.

7. Stay positive about weight loss

Virtually all people trying to lose weight will experience phases when they continue to stay at the same weight for what seems like a frustratingly long period of time. In actuality, it will probably be only a few weeks, and anecdotally 5:2 eaters seem to experience fewer plateaus, possibly because of the constant switch between higher and lower calorie intakes and because levels of lean tissue (with a higher energy expenditure than fat) are maintained. However, if you do experience a plateau, a positive mindset is key. Try to focus on the weight you have lost and consider every week that you stick with your fast days as a success that's worth patting yourself on the back for. In reality, it's only plateaus that happen early on that tend to be a problem. Most established 5:2 fans are so wedded to their routine, weight loss becomes purely a bonus. On a practical level, increasing your activity level a little can help shake you out of a plateau.

8. Keep busy

The devil may make work for idle hands, but you're also more likely to end up with your hands in the cookie jar if you're bored or not very busy. Part of planning a successful fasting day is, therefore, thinking what you will do to occupy yourself as well as what you will eat. The most successful days are those when you have particularly engrossing work project, are focusing on caring for children, or (hopefully from time to time) just enjoying a day out.

9. Get more sleep

The evidence that insufficient sleep correlates to higher body weight has been piling up, and the latest strand of evidence suggests junk food may be particularly appealing to tired brains. When scientists at St. Luke's-Roosevelt Hospital Center and Columbia University in New York used high-tech brain scans to measure responses to unhealthy foods (such as pepperoni pizza and candies) versus healthier options (oatmeal and fruit), they found that the brain's reward center lit up more at the sight of junk food if the subjects were fatigued.

The take-home message? Get plenty of sleep, particularly the night before a fast day. At the very least, it's good for your general well-being; at best, it may also help keep up your 5:2 resolve.

10. Don't be hard on yourself

If you have to miss a few fasting days because of vacations or other life events, don't be hard on yourself. There's always tomorrow or next week and you're meant to be living a life, not a life sentence!

YOUR RELATIONSHIPWITH FOOD

As time goes by, you can expect your relationship with food to change. Instead of food being your master, as is so often the case with those who have struggled with their weight over the years, you will probably notice a welcome shift in the locus of control, putting you in the driving seat once more. A frequent comment from people who adopt 5:2 as a lifestyle choice is that when they discover they can "crack" fast days, it is extremely empowering.

In essence, 5:2 fast days can help you to be more in tune with your body and its appetite and hunger cues. The confidence boost that this gives means a healthier relationship with food can develop. For some people, this will be more of an epiphany than others but, regardless of the magnitude of the effect, feeling more in control of your diet is always welcome.

5:2 for life

Once you've reached the weight you're happy with, what next? As you've read through these pages, I hope you've become convinced that intermittent fasting, or 5:2, could well be something you incorporate into your life long term, as an active lifestyle choice. When bigger, longer studies into intermittent fasting emerge, as they undoubtedly will, the optimal way to continue intermittent fasting so that you can maximize any health benefits and keep your weight maintained will almost certainly become more apparent.

For now, the consensus approach from most people doing 5:2 who have already reached their ideal weight and don't want to become any thinner is to switch to 500- or 600-calorie fasting just one day a week (a 6:1 diet). A small study showed people who had lost weight could keep it off by doing this, although another approach, if you want to keep a slightly firmer watch on your weight, would be to continue with two fast days—but let them creep up to 700 calories, say.

Some people may find they can manage by using 5:2 fasting now and again (that would be intermittent intermittent fasting), or to stop for longer periods or even altogether. These folks will be the ones who have become confident that they can now trust their own eating intuition to keep them safe from weight gain. In short, they can now trust their inbuilt hunger and fullness mechanisms (that were there all the time) to stay happily at their optimum weight.

Whatever your approach, remember that you should always obtain pleasure from your eating, and your diet should never become a terrible chore. If you choose intermittent fasting as your ongoing method of optimizing health and weight, the recipes and suggested plans that follow should make that eminently possible, for as long as you choose.

Frequently asked questions

How can I check my BMI?

The Body Mass Index (BMI) is an estimate of health risk based
on your height and weight. You can use an online calculator
(for example, at www.nhibisupport.com/bmi/) or work it out using
the following calculation. Measure your weight in pounds, divide it
by your height in inches squared, and multiply by 703. For example,
a woman of 5 feet 3 inches (63 inches) who weighs 140 pounds has
a BMI of 140 ÷ (63 × 63) x 703 = 24.8.

According to World Health Organization guidelines, a healthy BMI
is in the range of 18.5 to 25, with health risk starting to rise above this.
However, significant health risk probably does not kick in for many
until around 35. If you're short or of Asian descent, having a BMI above
the healthy range is more of a worry than if you're tall or athletic.

How does alternate day fasting compare?

Alternate day fasting is the type more widely researched in humans,
and in clinical studies has involved giving individuals meals set at
25 percent of their needs one day and 125 percent the next. There are
no direct comparisons of 5:2 fasting versus alternate day fasting, but
5:2 is just a logical adaptation that also works, and for very obvious
reasons is much less disruptive to people's lives.

Do some 5:2 diets suggest specific foods on fast day?

Yes, they do—the intermittent diet formulated by experts at the
Genesis Breast Cancer Prevention charity recommends that women
needing to lose weight should stick to protein and dairy foods,
vegetables, and one portion of fruit on their fast days (plus plenty
of calorie-free fluids). The diet has been proven clinically effective
at reducing weight and associated breast cancer risk. Find more
details at http://www.genesisuk.org.

Can I use 5:2 to lose a small amount of weight?

Yes—many people use the 5:2 diet to lose that slight increase in
weight that has crept on as they've got older, or to get back to a
lighter weight within the normal range that they feel happier with.
However, if you only have a small amount of weight to lose, you'll
lose it more slowly than if you have a lot to lose. And it goes without
saying that you shouldn't lose weight if it's going to move you out
of the bottom of the healthy BMI range (see above).

How tough will 5:2 be?

Everyone is different, and it can depend on everything from your genes to your mood on a particular day. The only way is to try it and you may be pleasantly surprised. You do, after all, eat *something*, and it can be surprising how filling 500 or 600 calories are when you start making the right food choices. Many people report that hunger becomes less and they no longer get hunger pangs midmorning or midafternoon once they have been doing 5:2 for a while.

Will my body go into "starvation mode"?

Starvation mode as it's popularly understood is something of a myth. In the context of most dieters' experiences, all it means is that your metabolic rate will decrease slightly as your body adapts to consistently fewer calories coming into the system.

Starvation mode is itself never responsible for weight gain (only increasing your calories again will do that) and is only really troublesome if you fast or drastically cut calories for long periods, in which case you will not achieve as great a weight loss as you might expect. On a 5:2 diet, the constant shake-up of low and higher calorie days will probably (although not proven) make starvation mode even less of a problem.

Can a fast day be any 24-hour period?

It could be, and doing it from 2 p.m. to 2 p.m. is one possibility that some people like. If you do this, you can have lunch as your final "off" day meal and then any combination of dinner and breakfast or lunch in the following 24-hour period as your two fast meals. You have to be sure not to overcompensate with your nonfast meals, however, because the timings can make this slightly more likely.

Won't I be so hungry that I just pig out on my "off" days?

No, this is not what the scientific evidence or ordinary people's experiences show. Dr. Krista Varady, an alternate day fasting expert, expected that her study subjects would eat around 175 percent of normal calories the day following a fast, but consistently she found this not to be true. Dr. Michelle Harvie also found her subjects, on a 5:2 diet, did not overcompensate.

Can I really eat cake on my "off" days?

No foods are banned, so yes. In fact, you can eat anything you want on either fast or nonfast days, but portions will have to be different and you soon learn that junk food calories don't go very far. If you consistently eat high-calorie foods on "off" days, then you'll get to the point where you outweigh the benefit of fast days, but this doesn't usually happen and the expectation is that you'll naturally start to crave healthier meals and not want to eat cake as much in any case.

Can I have alcohol?

On "off" days, yes. However, it's a bad idea on all kinds of levels on your fast days. Apart from containing a lot of calories, booze can lower your inhibition and self-control, leading you astray much more easily than would otherwise be the case.

Can I follow 5:2 for health and not to lose weight?

Yes, if you want to, but in this case it's probably best to have only one fast day a week. There's some (only scant) evidence that if you're just after the health benefits and not bothered about weight loss, eating all your fast day calories in just one meal at lunch or dinner could be better to extend the food-free period (see pages 11 and 17). However, don't do this if it feels in any way uncomfortable.

Can I sit down and eat with my family?

Yes—for example, you could just have a smaller portion or swap some of the pasta or rice for salad, or any similar trick that keeps you at the right calorie figure. Many of our recipes could be served to all the family with other family members having another accompanying dish. Cooking for other people and being around them when they eat may seem hard, but it can be surprisingly manageable when you're suitably focused. Most 5:2 eaters are, because they know that tomorrow they can be digging in with everybody else.

Just one word of caution if you have children: Kids learn food habits from their parents, so if you must tell them you're doing something different, explain that you're just enjoying really healthy food to satisfy your appetite instead of being "on a diet." Having children is one really good reason to carry through healthier eating habits into your "off" days, too.

4-week fast day meal planner

Tasty meals are your absolute ally on fast day, so here's a month's worth to get you started (or shake things up a little if you're getting stuck for ideas). Make sure you are scrupulous with portion sizes when you're serving up the recipes.

Week 1

DAY 1
- **Breakfast:** 1 poached egg on half a slice of whole-wheat toast spread with 1 teaspoon of low-fat spread and 1 medium (3 ounces) tomato, broiled (163 calories)
- **Lunch/Snack:** 1 rounded tablespoon (1 ounce) of tzatziki or nonfat Greek yogurt with 1 cup (3½ ounces) cucumber and red bell pepper sticks (60 calories)
- **Dinner:** Thai Noodles with Tofu (see page 140; 276 calories)

TOTAL 499 calories

If you're a man: Add 2 tablespoons (½ ounce) of plain peanuts to the Thai Noodles

DAY 2
- **Breakfast:** Red Fruit Salad (see page 67) with ¼ cup (2 ounces) nonfat Greek yogurt (132 calories)
- **Lunch/Snack:** 2 clementines (44 calories)
- **Dinner:** Broiled Sea Bass with Cherry Tomatoes (see page 122), with steamed broccoli and spinach and 2 small (2½ ounces) boiled new potatoes in their skins (330 calories)

TOTAL 506 calories

If you're a man: Add a bowl of 1¼ cups (10 ounces) of store-bought fresh carrot and cilantro soup at lunch

Week 2

DAY 1
- **Breakfast:** ¾ cup (1 ounce) serving of bran flakes with ½ cup low-fat milk and ½ cup (3 ounces) of blueberries (180 calories)
- **Lunch/Snack:** Watermelon & Feta Salad (see page 61; 99 calories)
- **Dinner:** Lentil & Pea Soup (see page 72) and half a slice of whole-wheat toast spread with 1 teaspoon of low-fat spread (208 calories)

TOTAL 497 calories

If you're a man: Serve yourself a bigger bowl of cereal (1½ cups/ 2 ounces bran flakes and ¾ cup low-fat milk) at breakfast

DAY 2
- **Breakfast:** ½ plain bagel topped with 2 tablespoons (1 ounce) light cream cheese and 2 ounces smoked salmon (270 calories)
- **Lunch/Snack:** 1 slice of cantaloupe and a clementine (45 calories)
- **Dinner:** Beef Skewers with Dipping Sauce (see page 91) and a dessert bowl of undressed green leaf, bell pepper, and tomato salad (174 calories)

TOTAL 504 calories

If you're a man: Top the melon with 2–3 slices of prosciutto

Week 3

DAY 1
- **Breakfast:** Oatmeal made with ½ cup (2 ounces) oats and 1 cup skimd milk, plus ⅔ cup (3 ounces) raspberries. Add sweetener, if desired (269 calories)
- **Lunch/Snack:** 1 large plum (about 3½ ounces; 31 calories)
- **Dinner:** 2 Lemon Grass Fish Skewers (see page 58) served with a large vegetable "steam-fry" (7 ounces bell pepper, cabbage, onions, and zucchini stir-fried in 1 teaspoon of oil and a few drops of water. Add soy sauce to taste (199 calories)

TOTAL 499 calories

If you're a man: Add half a slice of toast spread with 2 teaspoons of peanut butter

DAY 2
- **Breakfast:** 1 boiled egg with half a slice of whole-wheat toast spread with yeast extract (153 calories)
- **Lunch/Snack:** 1¼ cups (10 ounces) store-bought fresh carrot and cilantro soup and 1 smallish apple (about 3½ ounces; 150 calories)
- **Dinner:** Moroccan Tomato & Chickpea Salad (see page 76; 200 calories)

TOTAL 484 calories

If you're a man: Enjoy a serving of Mango & Lychee Mousse (see page 68)

Week 4

DAY 1
- **Breakfast:** 1 slice of whole-wheat toast spread with 1 teaspoon of low-fat spread and yeast extract, and ¾ cup (3½ ounces) of raspberries (147 calories)
- **Lunch/Snack:** 3½ ounces canned skinless, boneless sardines in tomato sauce on a bed of bagged salad greens, and 6 (3½ ounces) cherry tomatoes (183 calories)
- **Dinner:** Sweet Potato & Cabbage Soup (see page 74;160 calories)

TOTAL 490 calories

If you're a man: Have the sardines on a slice of toast

DAY 2
- **Breakfast:** 1 slice (1 ounce) of premium dry-cured ham and 1 slice (¾ ounce) of Jarlsberg cheese on 1 rye crispbread, and 1 clementine (175 calories)
- **Lunch/Snack:** 1 rounded tablespoon (1 ounce) of tzatziki or nonfat Greek yogurt with 1 cup (3½ ounces) cucumber and red bell pepper sticks (60 calories)
- **Dinner:** Vegetable Curry (see page 139) served with watercress leaves (270 calories)

TOTAL 505 calories

If you're a man: Have 2 plain poppadums with the curry

Snacks and treats

50 snacks up to 100 calories

- 1 whole medium (4 ounces) apple: 53 calories
- about 9 (½ ounce) plain almonds: 88 calories (weigh them because they vary)
- 1 warm crumpet spread with yeast extract (no butter): 100 calories
- 2 cups (½ ounce) salted popcorn: 83 calories
- 3½ ounces store-bought lemon and cilantro shrimp: 80 calories
- 1 slice of prosciutto wrapped around a breadstick: 58 calories
- 1 rye crispbread with 2 tablespoons (1 ounce) light cream cheese: 82 calories
- 1 individually wrapped mini malt loaf (for lunch bags): 95 calories
- 2 ounces reduced-fat shrimp cocktail: 83 calories
- 1½ tablespoons (½ ounce) roasted, salted peanuts: 89 calories
- 1 rounded tablespoon (1 ounce) of tzatziki or nonfat Greek yogurt with 1 cup (3½ ounces) cucumber and red bell pepper sticks: 60 calories
- scant ½ cup (3½ ounces) fat-free strawberry yogurt: 79 calories
- 1 light cheese triangle and 1 slice of cucumber spread on 1 oat cake or rice cake: 82 calories
- 1 medium banana: 95 calories
- ¾ cup (7 ounces) canned lentil soup: 95 calories
- 1 falafel with 1 teaspoon of sweet chili sauce: 65 calories
- ½ cup (3 ounces) cooked chicken tikka breast pieces: 90 calories
- 1 cold vegetarian sausage: 86 calories
- 1 vegetarian chicken nugget with 2 teaspoons of sweet chili dipping sauce: 87 calories
- about 2 (½ ounce) Brazil nuts: 82 calories (weigh them because they vary)
- ¾ ounce wafer-thin ham, 1 tomato, and a little mustard: 81 calories
- ⅔ cup low-fat strawberry milk shake: 90 calories
- ½ pomegranate: 55 calories
- 1 sesame rice cake with ½ tablespoon (¼ ounce) tahini: 74 calories
- 3 ounces store-bought cooked tikka-flavored chicken breast fillets: 98 calories
- 1 slice of fruit loaf: 98 calories
- ¼ cup (2 ounces) mashed avocado flesh sprinkled with lime juice: 100 calories
- 3½ tablespoons (2 ounces) reduced-fat hummus with cucumber sticks: 100 calories
- 1 package of cheesy-flavored corn puffs from a multipack: 96 calories
- 1 package of baked cheese-flavor corn puffs from a variety pack: 83 calories
- 1 slice of garlic bread: 95 calories

- 1 container of fat-free probiotic yogurt drink and 1 apple (3½ ounces): 78 calories
- 5 small strawberries topped with 2 rounded tablespoons (2½ ounces) of nonfat Greek yogurt with honey: 83 calories
- 1 fish stick with a serving of ketchup: 80 calories
- 1 mini gouda-type cheese: 61 calories
- 2 water crackers spread with 1 tablespoon of squeezy guacamole: 84 calories
- 2 cups (1½ ounces) arugula dressed with 2 tablespoons of low-fat balsamic dressing and 2 tablespoons (⅓ ounce) freshly grated Parmesan cheese: 71 calories
- ½ cup (1½ ounces) marinated olives: 85 calories
- 1 individual package of mini rye crispbreads: 90 calories
- 2 clementines and 1 kiwi: 73 calories
- Half a slice of toast, cut into sticks to dip into 3 tablespoons (2 ounces) mild salsa from a jar: 66 calories
- 1 hard-boiled egg: 84 calories
- 1 cup (2½ ounces) sun-dried tomatoes in oil, drained, served on a bed of salad greens: 87 calories
- ¼ cup (1 ounce) unshelled pistachio nuts: 86 calories
- 1 medium orange: 59 calories
- 1-ounce piece of Edam cheese: 85 calories
- 1 large rectangular or two 2½-inch square graham crackers: 59 calories
- 1¼ cups (10 ounces) store-bought fresh carrot and cilantro soup: 89 calories (they vary, so check the label)
- 1½ ounces canned tuna in water mashed with 3 tablespoons (1 ounce) canned corn kernels and 1 teaspoon of reduced-fat mayonnaise: 92 calories
- 1 store-bought lemon and raisin pancake: 88 calories

50 snacks up to 50 calories

- ½ cup (3 ounces) mango cubes: 46 calories
- 1 teaspoon of peanut butter spread on a celery stick: 42 calories
- 1 slice of cantaloupe: 23 calories
- ¾ cup (3½ ounces) frozen berries with sweetener: 30 calories
- 1 (3 ounces) apple and grape snack container: 45 calories
- 3 seafood sticks: 50 calories
- 2 clementines: 44 calories
- 1 large (3 ounces) crunchy whole carrot: 28 calories
- 1 small (3½ ounces) apple: 42 calories
- 3 (1 ounce) dried apricots: 38 calories (weigh them—they vary)

- ²/₃ cup (3½ ounces) fresh blackberries: 25 calories
- ½ cup (2½ ounces) fresh unpitted cherries: 23 calories
- 2 ounces cooked jumbo shrimp with a squeeze of lemon: 42 calories
- 1 gingersnap cookie: 47 calories
- 1 mini light Gouda-type cheese: 42 calories
- 2 slices of wafer-thin ham wrapped round a celery stick: 43 calories
- 1 rich tea cookie: 38 calories
- 1 oat cake or rice cake spread with yeast extract: 37 calories
- 1 cup (3½ ounces) cucumber sticks with 3 tablespoons (2 ounces) salsa from a jar: 26 calories
- ⅓ cup (2 ounces) red seedless grapes: 30 calories
- 6 (3½ ounces) cherry tomatoes: 20 calories
- 2 party-size chicken satay skewers: 36 calories
- 2 tablespoons (1 ounce) garlic and herb light cream cheese with celery sticks: 48 calories
- 1 envelope of miso soup with tofu: 30 calories
- 1 rounded tablespoon (1 ounce) of store-bought vegetable couscous salad: 48 calories
- Half a slice of Danish whole-wheat toast spread with 2 teaspoons of salmon paste: 45 calories
- 2 fresh apricots: 33 calories
- 1 water cracker topped with ⅓ ounce French chèvre: 65 calories
- 2 Melba toasts spread with 1 level teaspoon of reduced-sugar preserves: 34 calories
- 3½ ounces asparagus spears, steamed, with a shake of dried red pepper flakes: 28 calories
- 2 tablespoons of squeezy guacamole with celery sticks: 32 calories
- ½ medium banana: 47 calories
- 1 small bite-size sausage: 26 calories
- 1 regular cheese triangle: 43 calories
- 1½ cups (1½ ounces) bistro salad (mache, beet leaves, and Swiss chard) from a bag with 2½ tablespoons (½ ounce) pitted ripe black olives and 1 tablespoon of low-fat French dressing: 41 calories
- 2 cheddar cheese crackers: 44 calories
- 1 nectarine: 45 calories
- ½ pink grapefruit, with sweetener, if desired: 24 calories
- ½ red or orange bell pepper, cut into strips: 26 calories
- 2 teaspoons of toasted sunflower seeds: 42 calories
- 1 jumbo cheese-flavored rice and corn cake: 38 calories
- 6 slices (1 ounce) of bresaola: 48 calories
- 4 teaspoons (¾ ounce) relish with carrot sticks: 48 calories
- 1 mini pork salami sausage: 38 calories

- 2 prunes: 39 calories
- $^2/_3$ cup (3½ ounces) ripe papaya flesh: 43 calories

10 guilt-free treats

- 6 medium strawberries with ¼ cup (½ ounce) of aerosol cream: 85 calories
- 2 ounces gradvalax with sauce: 90 calories
- $^1/_3$ cup (6 ounces) prepared sugar-free cranberry and raspberry gelatin with $^2/_3$ cup (3 ounces) raspberries: 33 calories
- 2 tablespoons (½ ounce) cocoa-dusted almonds: 84 calories
- 1 slice of prosciutto with 3 watermelon balls: 48 calories
- 2 lumps (⅓ ounce) crystallized ginger: 37 calories
- 1 small juicy nectarine topped with 2 rounded tablespoons (2½ ounces) of nonfat Greek yogurt with honey: 95 calories
- 2 mini spring rolls: 90 calories.
- 2 poppadums: 100 calories
- 8 ounces store-bought shell-on mussels in garlic butter sauce: 75 calories

Recipes

100
CALORIES AND UNDER

Tahini hummus

- 1½ cups rinsed and drained canned chickpeas
- 2 tablespoons tahini
- 3 garlic cloves, chopped
- ½ cup lemon juice
- pinch of ground cumin
- vegetable stock or water (optional)
- paprika or chopped parsley, to garnish

1 Place the chickpeas, tahini, garlic, lemon juice, and cumin in a food processor or blender and process until well blended, adding a little water or vegetable stock if you prefer a thinner consistency. Add more garlic, lemon juice, or cumin to taste.

2 Transfer the hummus to a serving bowl and serve sprinkled with paprika or chopped parsley.

Top tip

To prepare for your fast day, shop in advance for all the ingredients you will need and try to make sure that there are no tempting snacks that might lead you astray.

69
CALORIES
PER SERVING

Serves 6
Preparation time 10 minutes, plus cooling
Cooking time 5 minutes

Jerusalem artichoke hummus

- 12 ounces Jerusalem artichokes, scrubbed
- 4 tablespoons butter, diced
- ⅔ cup chicken stock
- 1½ cups rinsed and drained canned chickpeas
- 1 teaspoon ground cumin
- 2 tablespoons lemon juice
- 1 garlic clove, crushed

1 Cook the artichokes in a saucepan of boiling water for 5 minutes or until tender. Drain and let cool.

2 Place the artichokes in a blender or food processor with the butter and stock and blend until smooth. Add the chickpeas, cumin, lemon juice, and garlic and blend again until smooth, then serve.

Top tip

It's possible to confuse hunger with thirst, so when you feel hungry, try drinking a large glass of water. To stay healthy and hydrated throughout the day, it is important to drink plenty of water.

Tomato & bell pepper salsa

- 4 (1 pound) tomatoes, finely chopped
- 1 green chile, finely chopped
- 1 red bell pepper, cored, seeded, and finely chopped
- grated rind and juice of 1 lime
- 2 tablespoons chopped parsley

1 Mix together all the ingredients in a small nonmetallic bowl. Let stand for 10 minutes to let the flavors develop before serving.

Top tip

Watch out for condiments. Replace ketchup, mayonnaise, or salad dressing with balsamic vinegar, mustard, or lemon juice, which have fewer calories.

Makes 12
Preparation time 15 minutes
Cooking time 20 minutes

Broccoli & spinach eggs

- 4 ounces (about ⅕ a bunch) broccoli
- 3½ cups (3½ ounces) baby spinach leaves
- 6 eggs
- 1¼ cups low-fat milk
- 2 tablespoons grated Parmesan cheese
- large pinch of ground nutmeg
- oil, for greasing
- salt and ground black pepper

1 Cut the broccoli into small florets and thickly slice the stems. Put in a steamer set over a saucepan of boiling water, cover, and cook for 3 minutes. Add the spinach and cook for another 1 minute or until the spinach has just wilted.

2 Beat together the eggs, milk, Parmesan cheese, nutmeg, and a little salt and black pepper in a bowl. Divide the broccoli and spinach among the sections of a lightly oiled deep 12-cup muffin pan, then pour in the egg mixture.

3 Bake in a preheated oven, at 375°F, for about 15 minutes or until lightly browned, well risen, and the egg mixture has set. Let cool in the pan for 1–2 minutes, then loosen the edges with a knife and turn out. Serve warm.

Makes 12
Preparation time 10 minutes, plus cooling
Cooking time 20–25 minutes

68
CALORIES
PER SERVING

Potato drop biscuits

- 4 large (1 pound 2 ounces) russet potatoes, peeled and cut into small chunks
- 1½ teaspoons baking powder
- 2 eggs
- ⅓ cup milk
- vegetable oil, for frying
- salt and ground black pepper

1 Cook the potatoes in a large saucepan of lightly salted boiling water for 15 minutes or until completely tender. Drain well, return to the pan, and mash until smooth. Let cool slightly.

2 Beat in the baking powder, then the eggs, milk, and a little salt and black pepper and continue to beat until everything is evenly combined.

3 Heat a little oil in a heavy skillet. Drop tablespoonfuls of the batter into the skillet, spacing them slightly apart, and sauté for 3–4 minutes, turning once, until golden. Transfer to a serving plate and keep warm. Repeat with the remaining potato batter to make 12 biscuits. (If broiling the potato biscuits, place tablespoonfuls of the mixture on an oiled, aluminum foil-lined baking sheet and cook under a preheated broiler for 5 minutes, turning once halfway through the cooking time.) Serve warm.

Smoked mackerel & chive pâté

- **7 ounces smoked mackerel, skinned, boned, and flaked**
- **½ cup low-fat cream cheese**
- **1 bunch of chives, chopped**
- **1 tablespoon fat-free vinaigrette**
- **1 tablespoon lemon juice**

1 Put the mackerel and cheese in a bowl and mash together well. Add the remaining ingredients and mix well. Alternatively, mix all the ingredients together in a food processor or blender.

2 Spoon the mixture into 8 small individual serving dishes or 1 large serving dish or mold. Cover and chill for at least 2 hours, or up to 4 hours, before serving.

Top tip

Try having an early night if you feel very hungry at the end of a fast day. Then you can go to sleep safe in the knowledge that you can have a hearty breakfast first thing in the morning.

Smoked salmon Thai rolls

- **12 slices of smoked salmon**
- **1 cucumber, peeled, seeded, and cut into matchsticks**
- **1 long red chile, seeded and thinly sliced**
- **handful each of cilantro, mint, and Thai basil leaves**

Dressing
- **2 tablespoons sweet chili sauce**
- **2 tablespoons honey**
- **2 tablespoons lime juice**
- **1 tablespoon Thai fish sauce**

1 Separate the smoked salmon slices and lay them flat on a work surface. Arrange the cucumber, chile, and herbs on the smoked salmon slices, placing an equal mound on each slice.

2 Make the dressing by combining all the ingredients in a screw-top jar, then drizzle it over the cucumber, chile, and herb filling.

3 Roll up the salmon slices to enclose the filling and dressing and serve.

Makes 8
Preparation time 5 minutes
Cooking time 4–5 minutes

Lemon grass fish skewers

- 8 ounces haddock or cod, boned, skinned, and cut into small pieces
- ½ tablespoon mint
- 1 tablespoon fresh cilantro leaves
- 1 teaspoon Thai red curry paste
- 1 lime leaf, finely chopped, or the rind of 1 lime
- 2 lemon grass stalks, quartered lengthwise
- oil, for brushing

1 Place the fish, mint, cilantro, curry paste, and lime leaf or rind in a blender or food processor and blend for 15–30 seconds, until well combined.

2 Divide the mixture into 8 and form each around a lemon grass stalk "skewer." Brush with a little oil and cook under a preheated hot broiler for 4–5 minutes, until cooked through. Serve immediately.

Makes 10
Preparation time 10 minutes, plus marinating
Cooking time 10 minutes

82
CALORIES
PER SERVING

Chicken satay

- **1 pound boneless, skinless chicken breast, cut into about 50 cubes**

Marinade
- **1 tablespoon smooth peanut butter**
- **½ cup soy sauce**
- **½ cup lime juice**
- **2 tablespoons curry powder**
- **2 garlic cloves, chopped**
- **1 teaspoon hot chili sauce**

1 Mix together the marinade ingredients in a nonmetallic bowl. Add the chicken and coat well. Cover and let marinate in the refrigerator for about 12 hours or overnight.

2 When ready to cook, thread about 5 cubes of chicken onto each of 10 skewers. Cook under a preheated hot broiler for 5 minutes on each side until cooked through. Serve hot.

Top tip

Plan your fasting days at the beginning of the week. It is a good idea to fast on days when you will be busy because you won't have so much time to think about food if you have a long list of things to get through.

Serves 4
Preparation time 15 minutes, plus chilling
Cooking time 25 minutes

Gazpacho

- 6 (1½ pounds) ripe tomatoes
- 1¼ cups water
- 1 large fennel bulb, trimmed and finely sliced
- ¾ teaspoon coriander seeds
- ½ teaspoon mixed peppercorns
- 1 tablespoon extra virgin olive oil
- 1 large garlic clove, crushed
- 1 small onion, chopped
- 1 tablespoon balsamic vinegar
- 1 tablespoon lemon juice
- ¾ teaspoon chopped oregano, plus extra leaves to garnish
- 1 teaspoon tomato paste
- 1 rounded teaspoon kosher salt
- finely sliced green olives, to garnish

1 Put the tomatoes in a large saucepan or heatproof bowl and pour in enough boiling water to cover them, then let stand for about 1 minute. Drain and skin the tomatoes carefully, then coarsely chop the flesh.

2 Put the measured water and a little salt in a saucepan and bring to a boil. Add the fennel, cover, and simmer for 10 minutes.

3 Meanwhile, crush the coriander seeds and peppercorns using a mortar and pestle. Heat the oil in a large saucepan, add the crushed spices, garlic, and onion, and cook gently for 5 minutes.

4 Add the vinegar, lemon juice, tomatoes, and chopped oregano. Stir well, then add the fennel with its cooking fluid, the tomato paste, and kosher salt. Bring to a simmer and cook for 10 minutes. Transfer the mixture to a food processor or blender and process together.

5 Cool the gazpacho, then cover and chill for at least several hours or preferably overnight. Serve garnished with oregano leaves and sliced olives.

Serves 4
Preparation time 10 minutes
Cooking time 2 minutes

99
CALORIES
PER SERVING

Watermelon & feta salad

- 1 tablespoon black sesame seeds
- 4 cups (1 pound) peeled, seeded, and diced watermelon
- 6 ounces feta cheese, diced
- 2½ handfuls of arugula
- handful of mint leaves

Dressing
- 2 tablespoons olive oil
- juice of ½ large lemon
- salt and ground black pepper

1 Dry-fry the sesame seeds in a small, nonstick skillet for a few minutes until aromatic, then set aside.

2 Arrange the watermelon and feta on a large serving plate with the arugula and mint.

3 Make the dressing by combining all the ingredients in a screw-top jar. Drizzle the dressing over the salad, sprinkle with the toasted sesame seeds, and serve.

Top tip

Make a list of the reasons why you are fasting and stick it on the front of your refrigerator. This will remind you of your goals whenever you reach for something to eat!

99
CALORIES
PER SERVING

Serves 4
Preparation time 10 minutes, plus cooling
Cooking time 10 minutes

Warm eggplant salad

- 2 tablespoons olive oil
- 2 small (2 pounds) eggplants, cut into small cubes
- 1 red onion, finely sliced
- 2 tablespoons capers, drained and coarsely chopped
- 4 (1 pound) tomatoes, chopped
- ¼ cup chopped parsley
- 1 tablespoon balsamic vinegar
- salt and ground black pepper

1 Heat the oil in a nonstick skillet, add the eggplants, and sauté for 10 minutes, until golden and softened.

2 Add the onion, capers, tomatoes, parsley, and vinegar and stir to combine. Season lightly with salt and black pepper. Remove from the heat and let cool for 10 minutes before serving.

Serves 4
Preparation time 10 minutes
Cooking time 10 minutes

93
CALORIES
PER SERVING

Garlic mushrooms with spinach & crispy bacon

- 8 open-cap mushrooms
- ¼ cup water
- scant 1 cup (7 ounces) extra-light garlic and herb cream cheese
- grated rind of 1 lemon
- 3½ cups (3½ ounces) baby leaf spinach
- 4 lean bacon strips, broiled until crisp, then coarsely chopped
- salt and ground black pepper

1 Put the mushrooms, gill sides up, in a large nonstick skillet with the measured water.

2 Mix together the cream cheese and lemon rind in a bowl, then season with salt and black pepper. Divide the mixture among the mushroom caps. Cover and cook over low heat for 5–6 minutes.

3 Layer the spinach over the mushrooms, replace the lid, and cook for another 2 minutes, until the spinach has wilted.

4 Divide the mushrooms among 4 warm serving plates, then top with the bacon and serve.

90
CALORIES
PER SERVING

Serves 4
Preparation time 10 minutes
Cooking time 25 minutes

Mushroom stroganoff

- 1 tablespoon canola oil
- 1 large onion, thinly sliced
- 4 celery sticks, thinly sliced
- 2 garlic cloves, crushed
- 8½ cups (1¼ pounds) coarsely chopped mixed mushrooms
- 2 teaspoons smoked paprika
- 1 cup vegetable stock
- ⅔ cup sour cream
- ground black pepper

1 Heat the oil in a nonstick skillet, add the onion, celery, and garlic, and cook for 5 minutes or until beginning to soften. Add the mushrooms and paprika and cook for another 5 minutes.

2 Pour in the stock and cook for another 10 minutes or until the liquid is reduced by half.

3 Stir in the sour cream and season with black pepper. Cook over medium heat for 5 minutes. Serve immediately.

Serves 4
Preparation time 15 minutes
Cooking time 25–30 minutes

44
CALORIES
PER SERVING

Ratatouille

- **2 large beefsteak tomatoes**
- **½ tablespoon olive oil**
- **1 small–medium (12 ounces) eggplant, cut into ½ inch chunks**
- **½ large Spanish onion, cut into ½ inch chunks**
- **2 celery sticks, coarsely chopped**
- **½ teaspoon chopped basil**

1 Put the tomatoes in a large saucepan or heatproof bowl and pour in enough boiling water to cover them, then let stand for about 1 minute. Drain, skin the tomatoes carefully, seed, and coarsely chop the flesh.

2 Heat the oil in a nonstick skillet until hot, add the eggplants, and sauté for about 10–15 minutes, until soft.

3 Meanwhile, put the onion and celery in a saucepan with a little water and cook for 3–5 minutes, until tender but still firm. Add the tomatoes and basil, then add the eggplant. Cook for 15 minutes, stirring occasionally. Serve hot.

Serves 4
Preparation time 10 minutes
Cooking time 15–20 minutes

Mushroom & pea bhaji

- 2 tablespoons vegetable oil
- ½ cup finely sliced onion
- ¼ teaspoon cumin seeds, crushed
- ¼ teaspoon mustard seeds
- 1 tomato, chopped
- 1 green chile, seeded and finely chopped
- 14 ounces button mushrooms, halved (or quartered if larger)
- 1 cup frozen peas
- ½ teaspoon chili powder
- ¼ teaspoon ground turmeric
- 1 red bell pepper, cored, seeded, and chopped
- 4 garlic cloves, crushed
- 2 tablespoons fresh cilantro leaves
- chopped scallions or chives, to garnish

1 Heat the oil in a saucepan, add the onion, and sauté gently for 2–3 minutes, until beginning to soften. Add the cumin and mustard seeds and sauté, stirring, for another 2 minutes.

2 Add the tomatoes, chile, mushrooms, and peas. Stir and cook for 2 minutes.

3 Add the chili powder and turmeric and mix well, then cook, uncovered, for another 5–7 minutes.

4 Add the red bell pepper, garlic, and cilantro and cook for 5 minutes, until the mixture is dry. Serve garnished with the scallions or chives.

100 CALORIES PER SERVING

Red fruit salad

- 1²⁄₃ cups (8 ounces) hulled fresh strawberries
- 2 cups (8 ounces) fresh raspberries
- 1²⁄₃ cups (8 ounces) seedless red grapes
- 1²⁄₃ cups (8 ounces) cubed watermelon
- 1 tablespoon balsamic vinegar
- ¼ cup port

1 Add the fruit to a bowl and mix, then add the vinegar and port and mix again.

2 Chill the fruit for 10–20 minutes before serving.

Top tip

Try drinking green tea. It contains no calories, is rich in antioxidants, and may even marginally increase your metabolic rate, giving you a slight weight-loss advantage.

Mango & lychee mousse

- 2⅓ cups canned mango slices in juice
- 2 cups canned lychees
- 2 tablespoons low-fat plain yogurt
- ¼ cup fromage blanc or nonfat Greek yogurt
- 1 teaspoon lime juice
- 1 tablespoon instant skim milk
- ½ teaspoon vanilla extract
- 2 teaspoons honey
- pared rind from unwaxed orange and lime, to decorate

1 Place all the ingredients except the pared rind in a blender or food processor and blend together. If you prefer a thicker consistency, add 1 extra tablespoon of instant skim milk.

2 Divide the mixture among 8 dessert glasses and chill for at least 30 minutes.

3 Decorate with a little pared orange and lime rind and serve.

Makes 30
Preparation time 10 minutes
Cooking time 5–6 minutes

30 CALORIES PER SERVING

Cranberry & hazelnut cookies

- 4 tablespoons unsalted butter, softened
- 3½ tablespoons granulated sugar
- 2 tablespoons firmly packed light brown sugar
- 1 egg, beaten
- a few drops of vanilla extract
- 1¼ cups all-purpose flour, sifted
- 1¼ teaspoons baking powder
- ½ cup rolled oats
- ⅓ cup dried cranberries
- ⅓ cup hazelnuts, toasted and chopped

1 Beat together the butter, sugars, egg, and vanilla extract in a large bowl until smooth. Stir in the flour, baking powder, and oats, then the dried cranberries and chopped hazelnuts.

2 Place teaspoonfuls of the dough on baking sheets lined with wax paper or nonstick parchment paper and flatten them slightly with the back of a fork.

3 Bake in a preheated oven, at 350°F, for about 5–6 minutes, until browned. Transfer to a wire rack and let cool. Store in an airtight container for up to 5 days.

Serves 6
Preparation time 10 minutes
Cooking time 7–8 minutes

Minted zabaglione with blueberries

- **4 egg yolks**
- **3 tablespoons light cane sugar**
- **½ cup sweet white wine or sherry**
- **1 cup blueberries, plus extra to decorate**
- **4 teaspoons chopped mint, plus extra to decorate**

1 Put the egg yolks and sugar in a large bowl set over a saucepan of simmering water. Use a handheld electric mixer or a wire whisk to beat the yolks and sugar for 2–3 minutes, until they are thick and pale.

2 Beat in the white wine or sherry, little by little, and continue beating for about 5 minutes, until the mixture is light, thick, and foaming.

3 Warm the blueberries in a small saucepan with 1 tablespoon of water and spoon them into the bottom of 6 small glasses. Beat the mint into the foaming wine mixture and pour it over the blueberries. Stand the glasses on small plates or on a tray and arrange a few extra berries around them. Top with a little chopped mint and serve immediately.

200
CALORIES
AND UNDER

Serves 4
Preparation time 10 minutes
Cooking time 2 hours

Lentil & pea soup

- 1 teaspoon olive oil
- 1 leek, trimmed and finely sliced
- 1 garlic clove, crushed
- 2 cups drained canned green lentils or cooked green lentils
- 2 tablespoons chopped fresh mixed herbs, such as thyme and parsley
- 1⅓ cups frozen peas
- 2 tablespoons crème fraîche or nonfat Greek yogurt
- 1 tablespoon chopped mint
- ground black pepper

Vegetable stock
- 1 tablespoon olive oil
- 1 onion, chopped
- 1 carrot, chopped
- 4 celery sticks, chopped
- any vegetable scraps, such as celery tops, onion skins, and tomato skins
- 1 bouquet garni
- 5¼ cups water
- salt and ground black pepper

1 To make the stock, heat the oil in a large saucepan, add the vegetables, and sauté for 2–3 minutes, then add the vegetable scraps and bouquet garni and season well. Pour in the measured water and bring to a boil, then reduce the heat and simmer gently for 1½ hours or until reduced to 3¾ cups. Drain over a bowl, discarding the vegetables and retaining the stock.

2 Heat the oil in a medium saucepan, add the leek and garlic, and sauté over low heat for 5–6 minutes, until the leek is softened.

3 Add the lentils, stock, and herbs and bring to a boil, then reduce the heat and simmer for 10 minutes. Add the peas and cook for another 5 minutes.

4 Transfer half the soup to a blender or food processor and blend until smooth. Return the blended soup to the pan, stir to combine with the unblended soup, then heat through and season with plenty of black pepper.

5 Stir together the crème fraîche and mint. Serve the soup topped with the crème fraîche.

Serves 4
Preparation time 15 minutes
Cooking time 35 minutes

155
CALORIES
PER SERVING

Fennel & white bean soup

- 3¾ cups vegetable stock
- 2 fennel bulbs, trimmed and chopped
- 1 onion, chopped
- 1 zucchini, chopped
- 1 carrot, chopped
- 2 garlic cloves, finely sliced
- 5 (1¼ pounds) tomatoes, finely chopped, or 1¾ cups canned tomatoes
- 4¾ cups rinsed and drained canned lima beans
- 2 tablespoons chopped sage
- ground black pepper

1 Pour 1¼ cups of the stock into a large saucepan. Add the fennel, onion, zucchini, carrot, and garlic, cover, and bring to a boil. Boil for 5 minutes, then remove the lid, reduce the heat, and simmer gently for about 20 minutes, until the vegetables are tender.

2 Stir in the tomatoes, beans, and sage. Season with black pepper and pour in the remaining stock. Simmer for 5 minutes, then let cool slightly.

3 Transfer 1¼ cups of the soup to a blender or food processor and blend until smooth. Return the blended soup to the pan, stir to combine with the unblended soup, and heat through gently before serving.

160
CALORIES
PER SERVING

Serves 4
Preparation time 15 minutes
Cooking time 25 minutes

Sweet potato & cabbage soup

- 2 onions, chopped
- 2 garlic cloves, sliced
- 4 lean bacon strips, chopped
- 3 (1 pound) sweet potatoes, peeled and chopped
- 2 parsnips, peeled and chopped
- 1 teaspoon chopped thyme
- 3¾ cups vegetable stock
- 1 baby savoy cabbage, shredded

1 Put the onions, garlic, and bacon in a large saucepan and sauté for 2–3 minutes. Add the sweet potatoes, parsnips, thyme, and stock and bring to a boil, then reduce the heat and simmer for 15 minutes.

2 Transfer two-thirds of the soup to a blender or food processor and blend until smooth. Return the blended soup to the pan, add the cabbage, and simmer for another 5–7 minutes, until the cabbage is just cooked.

Serves 4
Preparation time 5 minutes
Cooking time 20–25 minutes

160 CALORIES PER SERVING

Onion & fennel soup

- 1 tablespoon olive oil
- 6 onions, chopped
- 2 tablespoons chopped thyme
- 1 tablespoon rosemary leaves
- 5 cups vegetable stock or beef stock
- 2½ cups water
- 2 bulbs (14 ounces) trimmed fennel, finely sliced
- salt and ground black pepper
- Parmesan cheese shavings, to garnish

1 Heat the oil in a large saucepan over low heat, add the onions, thyme, and rosemary, and cook for 10 minutes.

2 Add the stock, measured water, and fennel and cook over medium heat for 10–15 minutes, or until the fennel is tender. Season with salt.

3 Serve the soup sprinkled with black pepper and garnished with Parmesan shavings.

Top tip

Soup is a great, low-calorie option when you want a filling lunch. Cook a big batch of soup in advance and freeze it in portions to defrost for a quick and easy lunch.

Serves 4
Preparation time 10 minutes, plus standing

Moroccan tomato & chickpea salad

- 1 red onion, finely sliced
- 4¾ cups rinsed and drained canned chickpeas
- 4 (1 pound) tomatoes, chopped
- ¼ cup lemon juice
- 1 tablespoon olive oil
- handful of fresh mixed herbs, such as mint and parsley, chopped
- pinch of paprika
- pinch of ground cumin
- salt and ground black pepper

1 Mix together all the ingredients in a large nonmetallic bowl and let stand for 10 minutes to let the flavors develop before serving.

Top tip

If you can't resist a taste of sweetness on your fast day, the best option would be to choose an airy dessert, such as a mousse, or a dish that uses fresh or dried fruit to provide the sweetness.

193 CALORIES PER SERVING

Tabbouleh salad

- 1¼ cups bulgur wheat
- 1¼ cups boiling water
- 1 red onion, finely chopped
- 3 tomatoes, diced
- ½ cucumber, chopped
- ⅔ cup chopped parsley
- ⅓ cup chopped mint

Dressing
- ½ cup lemon juice
- 2 teaspoons olive oil
- ground black pepper

1 Put the bulgur wheat in a bowl. Pour over the boiling water and let stand for 30 minutes, or according to the package directions, until the grains swell and soften.

2 Drain the bulgur wheat and press to remove the excess moisture. Put the bulgur wheat in a salad bowl with the onion, tomatoes, cucumber, parsley, and mint and toss to combine.

3 Make the dressing by combining all the ingredients in a screw-top jar. Pour over the salad, toss well, and serve.

Serves 6
Preparation time 15 minutes, plus standing
Cooking time 5 minutes

Orange & almond couscous salad

- 1 cup apple juice
- 1 cup couscous
- ½ red bell pepper, cored, seeded, and diced
- ¼ cup chopped parsley
- 3 tablespoons chopped mint
- 3 tablespoons dried currants
- 2 oranges
- 1 red onion, sliced
- ¼ cup slivered almonds

Dressing
- juice of 1 orange
- juice of 1 lemon or lime
- 2 teaspoons olive or hazelnut oil
- 1 teaspoon honey

1 Pour the apple juice into a saucepan and bring to a boil, then slowly stir in the couscous. Remove the pan from heat, cover, and let stand for 10 minutes. Fluff up with a fork.

2 Add the red bell pepper, herbs, and currants to the couscous and toss to combine. Transfer to a serving bowl.

3 Cut the top and bottom off the oranges with a serrated knife to reveal the flesh, then cut away the remaining peel and pith. Holding the fruit above the serving bowl, cut between the membranes to release the fruit segments over the couscous, then sprinkle with the onion.

4 To make the dressing, put all the ingredients in a small saucepan and heat gently to dissolve the honey—do not let boil. Drizzle the dressing over the salad and serve sprinkled with the almonds.

Serves 4
Preparation time 15 minutes, plus marinating
Cooking time 1 minute

178 CALORIES PER SERVING

Asian tuna salad

- 12 ounces tuna steak, cut into strips
- 3 tablespoons soy sauce
- 1 teaspoon wasabi paste
- 1 tablespoon sake or dry white wine
- 7 cups (7 ounces) mixed salad greens
- 8 yellow cherry tomatoes, halved
- 1 cucumber, sliced into wide, fine strips

Dressing
- 2 tablespoons soy sauce
- 1 tablespoon lime juice
- 1 teaspoon packed brown sugar
- 2 teaspoons sesame oil

1 Mix together the tuna, soy sauce, wasab,i and sake or white wine in a nonmetallic bowl. Let marinate for 10 minutes.

2 Arrange the salad greens, tomatoes, and cucumber on 4 serving plates.

3 Make the dressing by combining all the ingredients in a screw-top jar.

4 Heat a nonstick skillet over a high heat, add the tuna, and cook for about 10 seconds on each side or until seared. Place the tuna on top of the salad, drizzle with the dressing and serve.

144
CALORIES
PER SERVING

Serves 4
Preparation time 10 minutes, plus chilling
Cooking time 15–20 minutes

Chicken salad Thai style

- 1 cup (5 ounces) shredded cooked chicken breast
- 3 tablespoons cilantro leaves
- 2 cups shredded bok choy

Dressing
- 1 tablespoon peanut oil
- 1 tablespoon Thai fish sauce
- juice of 1 lime
- juice of 1 small orange
- 1 garlic clove, crushed
- 3 tablespoons coarsely chopped basil
- ground black pepper

To garnish
- 2 scallions, green stems only, shredded lengthwise
- 1 plump red chile, seeded and sliced diagonally

1 Make the dressing by combining all the ingredients in a screw-top jar.

2 Mix together the chicken and cilantro leaves in a bowl, then stir in the dressing.

3 Line a serving dish with the bok choy, spoon the dressed chicken on top, cover, and chill before serving. Serve garnished with scallion shreds and red chile slices.

Serves 4
Preparation time 5 minutes, plus soaking
Cooking time 4–5 minutes

199 CALORIES PER SERVING

Hot chicken liver salad

- **13 ounces chicken livers, trimmed and halved**
- **¼ cup milk**
- **2 teaspoons chopped thyme**
- **1 tablespoon olive oil**
- **2 garlic cloves, crushed**
- **1 red chile, thinly sliced (optional)**
- **7 ounces canned water chestnuts, drained and halved**

To serve

- **2 heads (7 ounces) endive, leaves separated**
- **1½–2 tablespoons balsamic vinegar**

1 Soak the chicken livers in the milk for 30 minutes to remove any bitterness. Discard the milk and pat the livers dry with paper towels. Sprinkle the thyme over both sides of the livers.

2 Heat the oil in a large skillet, add the garlic and chile, if using, and soften for 30 seconds. Add the chicken livers and water chestnuts and cook over medium heat for 3–4 minutes, until the livers are browned on the outside but still pink in the center.

3 Serve on a bed of crispy raw endive, drizzled with balsamic vinegar and any remaining pan juices.

Serves 4
Preparation time 10 minutes

Caprese salad

- 3 (1 pound) beefsteak tomatoes, sliced
- 2 balls of mozzarella cheese, sliced
- 3 tablespoons vinaigrette
- 2 tablespoons chopped basil
- salt and ground black pepper

1 Arrange the tomato and mozzarella in overlapping slices on a large serving plate.

2 Drizzle with the vinaigrette.

3 Sprinkle with the basil, season with salt and black pepper, and serve.

Top tip

Keep a record of everything you eat and drink in a food journal. This is a good way to make sure that you are staying within you calorie limit while still eating a balanced diet.

Serves 4
Preparation time 15 minutes, plus marinating
Cooking time 10 minutes

195
CALORIES
PER SERVING

Thai-style fish kebabs

- 1–1½ pounds firm white fish, such as monkfish, swordfish, cod, or haddock, cut into large cubes
- 1 zucchini, cut into 8 pieces
- 1 onion, quartered and layers separated
- 8 mushrooms
- vegetable oil, for brushing

Marinade
- grated rind and juice of 2 limes
- 1 garlic clove, finely chopped
- 2 tablespoons finely sliced fresh ginger root
- 2 chiles, seeded and finely chopped
- 2 lemon grass stalks, finely chopped
- handful of cilantro leaves, finely chopped
- 1 glass of red wine
- 2 tablespoons sesame oil
- ground black pepper

1 Mix together the marinade ingredients in a large nonmetallic bowl. Add the fish, zucchini, onion, and mushrooms and coat well. Cover and let marinate in the refrigerator for 1 hour.

2 Brush the rack of a broiler pan lightly with oil to prevent the kebabs from sticking. Thread 4 skewers alternately with the chunks of fish, mushrooms, zucchini, and onion. Brush with a little oil and cook under a preheated hot broiler for about 10 minutes, turning the skewers frequently, until cooked through. Serve hot.

199
CALORIES
PER SERVING

Serves 4
Preparation time 15 minutes, plus standing
Cooking time 5 minutes

Crab & noodle Asian wraps

- 7 ounces rice noodles
- 1 bunch of scallions, finely sliced
- ¾ inch piece of fresh ginger root, peeled and grated
- 1 garlic clove, finely sliced
- 1 red chile, finely chopped
- 2 tablespoons chopped cilantro
- 1 tablespoon chopped mint
- ¼ cucumber, cut into fine matchsticks
- 12 ounces canned crabmeat, drained, or 10 ounces fresh white crabmeat
- 1 tablespoon sesame oil
- 1 tablespoon sweet chili sauce
- 1 teaspoon Thai fish sauce
- 16 Chinese pancakes or Vietnamese rice paper wrappers

1 Cook the rice noodles according to the package directions. Drain, then refresh under cold running water.

2 Mix together all the remaining ingredients, except the pancakes or rice paper wrappers, in a large bowl. Add the noodles and toss to mix. Cover and let stand for 10 minutes to let the flavors develop, then transfer to a serving dish.

3 Allowing 4 per person, top the pancakes or rice paper wrappers with some of the crab-and-noodle mixture and roll up to eat.

Serves 6
Preparation time 25–30 minutes
Cooking time 10 minutes

185
CALORIES
PER SERVING

Crab & cilantro cakes

- 12 ounces canned crabmeat, drained
- 1 cup cold mashed potatoes
- 2 tablespoons chopped cilantro
- 1 bunch of scallions, finely sliced
- grated rind and juice of ½ lemon
- 2 eggs, beaten
- flour, for coating
- 3 cups fresh white bread crumbs
- 1 tablespoon vegetable oil

1 Mix together the crabmeat, mashed potatoes, cilantro, scallions, and lemon rind and juice in a large bowl, then add half the beaten egg to bind.

2 Form the mixture into 12 cakes about ½ inch thick. Coat the cakes with flour, then dip into the remaining egg and then the bread crumbs.

3 Heat the oil in a nonstick skillet, add the cakes, and sauté for about 10 minutes, until golden, turning once or twice. Remove from the skillet and drain on paper towels. Divide the crab cakes among 6 serving plates and serve hot.

Serves 4
Preparation time 30 minutes, plus marinating
Cooking time 3–5 minutes

Marinated shrimp & zucchini ribbons

- 2 (14½ ounces) zucchini, sliced into fine ribbons with a vegetable peeler
- 28 large shrimp, peeled but with tails still intact, heads removed
- chopped flat-leaf parsley, to garnish

Marinade
- large pinch of saffron threads
- ½ cup lemon juice
- 6 garlic cloves, coarsely chopped
- 2 tablespoons rice wine vinegar
- ¼ cup olive oil
- 2 tablespoons capers, drained

1 Mix together all the marinade ingredients, lightly crushing the capers against the side of the bowl. Spoon two-thirds of the marinade mixture on top of the zucchini ribbons in a large nonmetallic bowl. Cover and let marinate in the refrigerator for 3–4 hours.

2 Meanwhile, prepare the shrimp. Hold the tail, underside up, and cut each shrimp in half lengthwise. Pull out any black intestinal thread, rinse, pat dry, on paper towels, and place in a shallow nonmetallic dish. Alternatively, ask your fish dealer to prepare the shrimp for you. Pour the remaining marinade over the shrimp, cover, and let marinate in the refrigerator for 3–4 hours.

3 When ready to cook, put the zucchini in a large skillet with their marinade and simmer over medium-low heat for 3–5 minutes.

4 Meanwhile, cook the shrimp under a preheated broiler for 3–4 minutes, until pink and sizzling, basting with the marinade. Do not overcook them.

5 Pile the zucchini in the center of a warm serving dish, top with the shrimp, and serve garnished with chopped parsley.

Serves 4
Preparation time 10 minutes
Cooking time 10 minutes

182
CALORIES
PER SERVING

Pan-fried flounder with mustard sauce

- 1 teaspoon olive oil
- 1 small onion, finely chopped
- 1 garlic clove, crushed
- 4 flounder or sole fillets, about 5 ounces each
- ½ cup dry white wine
- 2 tablespoons whole-grain mustard
- scant 1 cup crème fraîche or nonfat Greek yogurt
- 2 tablespoons chopped fresh mixed herbs

1 Heat the oil in a large skillet, add the onion and garlic, and sauté for 3 minutes, until softened.

2 Add the fish fillets and cook for 1 minute on each side, then add the wine and simmer until reduced by half.

3 Stir through the remaining ingredients and bring to a boil, then reduce the heat and simmer for 3–4 minutes, until the sauce has thickened slightly and the fish is tender. Serve immediately.

Top tip

Reward yourself for your successes. Set yourself targets and, once you have reached them, treat yourself to something nice.

Serves 6
Preparation time 10 minutes, plus chilling (optional)
Cooking time 5 minutes

Parsley & garlic sardines

- 12 fresh sardines, cleaned, or use fillets if preferred

Marinade
- ¾ cup chopped parsley
- 1 teaspoon ground black pepper
- 1 garlic clove, crushed
- finely grated rind and juice of 1 lemon
- 2 tablespoons white wine
- 1 tablespoon olive oil

1 Put all the marinade ingredients in a small saucepan and bring to a boil, then remove from the heat.

2 Place the sardines on a hot barbecue grill or on a preheated hot ridged grill pan or under a hot broiler. Cook for 1–2 minutes on each side until crisp and golden.

3 Arrange the sardines in a single layer in a shallow serving dish. Pour the warm marinade over the sardines and serve hot. Alternatively, cover and chill for at least 1 hour before serving cold.

Serves 4
Preparation time 15 minutes, plus chilling
Cooking time 6–8 minutes

135 CALORIES PER SERVING

Chicken burgers with tomato salsa

- 1 garlic clove, crushed
- 3 scallions, finely sliced
- 1 tablespoon pesto
- 2 tablespoons chopped fresh mixed herbs, such as parsley, tarragon, and thyme
- 12 ounces ground chicken
- 2 sun-dried tomatoes, finely chopped
- 1 teaspoon olive oil

Tomato salsa
- 16 (8 ounces) cherry tomatoes, quartered
- 1 red chile, seeded and finely chopped
- 1 tablespoon chopped cilantro
- grated rind and juice of 1 lime

1 Mix together all the ingredients for the burgers except the oil. Divide the mixture into 4 and form neat, flattened patties. Cover and chill for 30 minutes.

2 Meanwhile, mix together all the tomato salsa ingredients in a bowl.

3 Lightly brush the burgers with the oil and cook under a preheated hot broiler or on a barbecue grill for 3–4 minutes on each side until cooked through. Serve immediately with the salsa.

133
CALORIES
PER SERVING

Makes 16
Preparation time 5 minutes, plus marinating
Cooking time 50 minutes

Sticky chicken drumsticks

- **16 chicken drumsticks**
- **4 tablespoons honey**
- **finely grated rind and juice of 1 lemon**
- **finely grated rind and juice of 1 orange**
- **3 tablespoons Worcestershire sauce**
- **¼ cup ketchup**

1 Make several diagonal cuts through the fleshy part of each chicken drumstick and arrange in a single layer in a shallow ovenproof dish.

2 Mix together the remaining ingredients and spoon the marinade over the chicken. Cover and let marinate in the refrigerator until ready to cook.

3 Bake in a preheated oven, at 350°F, for about 50 minutes, turning and basting frequently until the chicken is cooked through and thickly coated with the sticky glaze. Serve hot or chill thoroughly and serve cold.

Serves 4
Preparation time 10 minutes, plus marinating
Cooking time 2–3 minutes

140 CALORIES PER SERVING

Beef skewers with dipping sauce

- **11½ ounces lean top sirloin steak, cut into strips**

Marinade
- **1 tablespoon sweet chili sauce**
- **½ teaspoon cumin seeds, toasted (see page 61)**
- **½ teaspoon ground coriander**
- **1 teaspoon olive oil**

Dipping sauce
- **1 tablespoon sweet chili sauce**
- **1 teaspoon Thai fish sauce**
- **1 teaspoon white wine vinegar**

To garnish
- **2 tablespoons chopped cilantro**
- **1 tablespoon coarsely chopped unsalted peanuts (optional)**

1 Mix together the marinade ingredients in a nonmetallic bowl. Add the steak and stir well to coat, then cover and let marinate in the refrigerator for 30 minutes.

2 Thread the steak onto 4 wooden skewers that have been soaked in water for at least 20 minutes. Cook on a hot ridged grill pan or under a preheated hot broiler for 2–3 minutes, until cooked through.

3 Meanwhile, mix together the sauce ingredients in a small serving bowl. Serve the skewers with the dipping sauce, sprinkled with the chopped cilantro and peanuts, if desired.

Serves 6
Preparation time 20 minutes
Cooking time 25 minutes

Piperade with sofrito and pastrami

- **6 extra-large eggs**
- **thyme sprigs, leaves removed, or large pinch of dried thyme, plus extra sprigs to garnish**
- **1 tablespoon olive oil**
- **4 ounces pastrami, thinly sliced**
- **salt and ground black pepper**

Sofrito

- **3 small (12 ounces) different colored bell peppers**
- **4 (1 pound) tomatoes**
- **1 tablespoon olive oil**
- **1 onion, finely chopped**
- **2 garlic cloves, crushed**

1 To make the sofrito, broil or cook the bell peppers directly in a gas flame for about 10 minutes, turning them until the skins have blistered and blackened. Rub the skins from the flesh and discard. Rinse the bell peppers under cold running water. Halve and seed, then cut the flesh into strips.

2 Put the tomatoes into a large saucepan or heatproof bowl and pour in enough boiling water to cover them, then let stand for about 1 minute. Drain, skin the tomatoes carefully, and chop the flesh.

3 Heat the oil in a large skillet, add the onion, and cook gently for 10 minutes, until softened and transparent. Add the garlic, tomatoes, and black pepper and simmer for 5 minutes, until any juice has evaporated from the tomatoes. Set aside until ready to serve.

4 Beat together the eggs, thyme, and salt and black pepper in a bowl. Heat the oil in a saucepan, add the eggs, stirring until they are lightly scrambled.

5 Meanwhile, reheat the sofrito. Stir the scrambled eggs into the reheated sofrito and spoon onto 6 serving plates. Arrange slices of pastrami around the eggs and serve immediately, garnished with sprigs of thyme.

Serves 4
Preparation time 5 minutes
Cooking time 5–7 minutes

195
CALORIES
PER SERVING

Liver with Marsala sauce

- 1 tablespoon rice flour
- 1 pound liver, thinly sliced
- 1 tablespoon olive oil
- 2 tablespoons butter
- 1 garlic clove, chopped
- 2 teaspoons chopped sage, plus extra sprigs to garnish
- ½ cup chicken stock
- 3 tablespoons Marsala wine
- salt and ground black pepper

1 Place the flour on a plate and season with salt and black pepper, then coat the liver in the flour.

2 Heat the oil and butter in a large skillet, add the garlic and liver, and cook for 1–2 minutes on each side. Add the chopped sage and stock and cook for another 2 minutes. Remove the liver from the pan with a slotted spoon and keep warm on a serving dish.

3 Add the Marsala to the skillet and season with salt and black pepper. Bring the sauce to a boil, stirring continuously for 1 minute, then pour it over the liver and serve immediately, garnished with sprigs of sage.

Serves 4
Preparation time 5 minutes
Cooking time 13 minutes

Green beans with ham & garlic

- 4½ cups (1 pound) trimmed green beans
- 2 tablespoons olive oil
- 1 onion, sliced
- 1 garlic clove, crushed
- 3 ounces prosciutto or cured ham, cubed
- salt and ground black pepper

1 Cook the beans in a saucepan of salted boiling water for about 8 minutes, until almost tender.

2 Meanwhile, heat the oil in a skillet, add the onion, and sauté until softened. Add the garlic and ham and cook for 1 minute.

3 Drain the beans and add to the skillet, then cover and cook for 5 minutes. Season with salt and black pepper and serve.

Top tip

Find yourself a diet buddy. Dieting together can introduce a some healthy competition, and you can encourage each other when the going gets tough.

Serves 2
Preparation time 10 minutes
Cooking time 25 minutes

168
CALORIES
PER SERVING

Baked mushrooms & artichokes

- 1 pound canned artichoke hearts, drained
- 1 teaspoon olive oil, plus extra for greasing
- ½ onion, finely chopped
- 2 garlic cloves, finely chopped
- 4 cups (10 ounces) sliced mushrooms
- 1 tablespoon chopped basil
- 1 tablespoon chopped oregano
- 1 tablespoon lemon juice
- 1 tablespoon dry white wine
- 1 tablespoon whole-wheat bread crumbs
- 1 tablespoon grated Parmesan cheese
- salt and ground black pepper
- parsley sprigs, to garnish

1 Place the artichokes in a lightly oiled, medium baking pan.

2 Heat the oil in a medium, nonstick skillet over medium heat, add the onion and garlic, and sauté gently, stirring frequently, for 3 minutes. Stir in the mushrooms and herbs.

3 Add the lemon juice and wine, then season with salt and black pepper and cook for another 3 minutes. Remove from the heat and stir in the bread crumbs.

4 Spoon the mushroom mixture evenly over the artichokes, then bake in a preheated oven, at 350°F, for 10 minutes.

5 Remove from the oven and sprinkle with the Parmesan. Bake for another 10 minutes, then serve garnished with sprigs of parsley.

Serves 4
Preparation time 10 minutes
Cooking time 20–25 minutes

Baked vegetable frittata

- 8 ounces asparagus, trimmed and halved
- 1 tablespoon extra virgin olive oil
- 2 leeks, trimmed and sliced
- 2 garlic cloves, crushed
- 2 tablespoons chopped basil
- 6 eggs
- 2 tablespoons milk
- butter, for greasing
- 2 tablespoons grated Parmesan cheese
- salt and ground black pepper

1 Cook the asparagus in a saucepan of lightly salted boiling water for 2 minutes, drain, and shake dry.

2 Meanwhile, heat the oil in a large skillet, add the leeks and garlic, and sauté gently for 5 minutes or until softened. Add the asparagus and basil and remove the pan from the heat.

3 Beat together the eggs and milk in a bowl and season with salt and black pepper. Stir in the vegetable mixture and pour into a greased 1¼-quart ovenproof dish.

4 Sprinkle with the Parmesan and bake in a preheated oven, at 400°F, for 15–20 minutes, until firm in the center. Serve immediately.

Serves 6
Preparation time 10 minutes
Cooking time 30–35 minutes

200 CALORIES PER SERVING

Zucchini & mint frittatas with tomato sauce

- 1 tablespoon olive oil, plus extra for greasing
- 1 onion, finely chopped
- 2 small (12 ounces) zucchini, halved lengthwise and thinly sliced
- 6 eggs
- 1¼ cups milk
- 3 tablespoons grated Parmesan cheese
- 2 tablespoons chopped mint, plus extra leaves to garnish (optional)
- salt and ground black pepper

Tomato sauce
- 1 tablespoon olive oil
- 1 onion, finely chopped
- 1–2 garlic cloves, crushed (optional)
- 8 (1 pound) plum tomatoes, chopped

1 To make the sauce, heat the oil in a saucepan, add the onion, and sauté for 5 minutes, stirring occasionally until softened and just beginning to brown. Add the garlic, if using, and tomatoes and season with salt and black pepper. Stir and simmer for 5 minutes, until the tomatoes are soft. Transfer to a blender or food processor and blend until smooth, then pass the sauce through a fine strainer into a bowl and keep warm.

2 Heat the oil in a skillet, add the onion, and sauté until softened and just beginning to brown. Add the zucchini, stir to combine, and cook for 3–4 minutes, until softened but not browned.

3 Beat together the eggs, milk, Parmesan, and mint in a small bowl, then stir in the zucchini and season well. Pour the mixture into the sections of a lightly oiled 12-cup muffin pan.

4 Bake in a preheated oven, at 375°F, for about 15 minutes, until lightly browned, well risen, and the egg mixture has set. Let cool in the pan for 1–2 minutes, then loosen the edges with a knife and turn out.

5 Place 2 frittatas on each of 6 serving plates. Serve with the warm tomato sauce, garnished with mint leaves, if desired.

Serves 4
Preparation time 30 minutes
Cooking time 12 minutes

Vietnamese vegetable spring rolls with plum sauce

- ¼ head (7 ounces) bok choy
- 2 tablespoons sunflower oil
- 1 small (3½ ounces) sweet potato, peeled and cut into matchstick strips
- 2 small (3½ ounces) carrots, cut into matchstick strips
- ½ bunch of scallions, cut into matchstick strips
- ½ cup bean sprouts,
- 2 garlic cloves, finely chopped
- ¾ inch piece of fresh ginger root, peeled and finely chopped
- 8 rice pancakes
- bunch of cilantro

Plum sauce
- 4 (8 ounces) ripe red plums, pitted and chopped
- 2 tablespoons water
- 1 tablespoon soy sauce
- 1 tablespoon superfine or granulated sugar
- made-up wasabi, to taste

1 Cut the leaves from the bok choy and slice the stems into matchstick strips. Heat 1 tablespoon of the oil in a wok or large skillet, add the sweet potato and carrot, and stir-fry for 2 minutes. Add the scallions and boy choy stems and cook for 1 minute. Mix in the bean sprouts, garlic, and ginger and cook for 1 minute. Transfer to a bowl.

2 Heat the remaining oil in the pan, add the bok choy leaves, and cook for 2–3 minutes, until just wilted.

3 Dip a rice pancake into a bowl of hot water and let stand for 20–30 seconds, until softened. Lift out and place on a clean dish towel. Top with a bok choy leaf, one-eighth of the vegetable mixture, and 2 stems of cilantro. Fold in the pancake edges and roll up tightly. Repeat with the remaining pancakes to make 8 spring rolls. Cover with plastic wrap and set aside. Serve within 1 hour.

4 Meanwhile, make the sauce. Put the plums in a small saucepan with the measured water, cove,r and cook for 5 minutes, until softened. Puree the plums with the soy sauce in a food processor, then mix in the sugar and wasabi to taste.

5 Garnish the spring rolls with the remaining sprigs of cilantro and serve 2 per person with small bowls of the sauce.

Serves 4
Preparation time 15 minutes
Cooking time 8–10 minutes

122 CALORIES PER SERVING

Grilled eggplants with chili toasts

- 2 teaspoons olive oil
- 2 small (1 pound 2 ounces) eggplants, cut into ¼ inch slices lengthwise
- 1 cup sun-dried tomatoes
- 2 garlic cloves, crushed
- ¼ cup lemon juice
- ground black pepper
- 4 basil leaves, to garnish

Chili toasts
- 4 slices of multigrain bread
- 1 tablespoon chili-infused oil

1 To make the chili toasts, remove the crusts from the bread, then cut each slice into 2 neat triangles. Brush each side of the bread with chili-infused oil and place the bread on a baking sheet. Place in a preheated oven, at 425°F for 8–10 minutes, until crisp and golden.

2 Meanwhile, heat the oil in a ridged grill pan. Season the eggplant slices with black pepper and add to the pan with the sun-dried tomatoes and garlic and cook for about 4 minutes, until beginning to soften. Turn the eggplants over and cook for another 4 minutes, then add the lemon juice.

3 Remove the chili toasts from the oven and serve with the eggplant and tomatoes piled high in the center of 4 serving plates, seasoned with pepper and garnished with the basil leaves.

Serves 4
Preparation time 30 minutes
Cooking time 1½ hours

Stuffed red onions

- 4 large red onions, peeled
- 2 tablespoons olive oil
- 1¾ cups (4 ounces) finely chopped button mushrooms
- ½ cup bulgur wheat
- 1 tablespoon chopped parsley
- 1¼ cups water
- 1 tablespoon golden raisins
- 1 tablespoon grated Parmesan cheese (optional)
- salt and ground black pepper

1 Cut the top off each onion and scoop out the center using a teaspoon, then finely chop the scooped-out onion. Heat the oil in a skillet, add the chopped onion, and sauté until softened and golden brown. Add the mushrooms and cook, stirring, for another 5 minutes.

2 Meanwhile, bring a large saucepan of water to a boil, add the onion cups, and simmer for 10 minutes or until they begin to soften. Drain well.

3 Add the bulgur wheat, parsley, salt, black pepper, and measured water to the mushrooms and boil for 5 minutes, then reduce the heat, cover, and simmer for another 30 minutes or until the grains have softened, adding extra water, if necessary. Stir in the golden raisins, then spoon the bulgur mixture into the onion cups.

4 Place the onions in a roasting pan and cover with aluminum foil. Bake in a preheated oven, at 375°F, for 30 minutes.

5 Remove from the oven and take off the foil. Sprinkle with the Parmesan, if using, and bake for another 10 minutes. Serve hot.

Serves 6
Preparation time 5 minutes
Cooking time 30 minutes

170
CALORIES
PER SERVING

Quick red onion tagine

- ⅓ cup olive oil
- 3 (1½ pounds) red onions, finely sliced
- pinch of saffron threads
- ¼ teaspoon ground ginger
- 1 teaspoon ground black pepper
- ½ teaspoon ground cinnamon
- 1 tablespoon packed brown sugar
- ⅔ cup red wine
- chopped parsley or cilantro, to garnish

1 Heat the oil in a skillet, add the onions, saffron, ginger, black pepper, cinnamon, and sugar and cook over high heat for 2–3 minutes, stirring continuously. Add the red wine, continuing to stir, and boil rapidly until reduced to a syrupy consistency.

2 Transfer the onion mixture to a heavy casserole dish and cover with aluminum foil. Place in a preheated oven, at 400°F, for 20 minutes.

3 Remove from the oven and take off the foil, then bake for another 5 minutes or until the onions are lightly glazed. Sprinkle with a little chopped parsley or cilantro and serve hot or cold.

147
CALORIES
PER SERVING

Serves 6
Preparation time 15 minutes
Cooking time 35–40 minutes

Spicy roasted vegetables

- 1 teaspoon fennel seeds
- 1 teaspoon cumin seeds
- 1 teaspoon coriander seeds
- ½ teaspoon ground turmeric
- ½ teaspoon paprika
- 2 garlic cloves, chopped
- 3 tablespoons olive oil
- ½ (1 pound) butternut squash, peeled, halved, seeded, and thickly sliced
- 4 small (14 ounces) parsnips, cut into quarters
- 3 (10 ounces) carrots, cut into thick strips
- salt and ground black pepper

1 Crush the seeds using a mortar and pestle or the end of a rolling pin. Transfer to a large plastic bag and add the turmeric, paprika, garlic, oil, and salt and black pepper. Squeeze the bag to mix the contents together.

2 Add the vegetables to the plastic bag, grip the top edge to seal, and toss together until the vegetables are coated with the spices.

3 Tip the vegetables into a roasting pan and bake in a preheated oven, at 400°F, for 35–40 minutes, turning once until browned and tender. Serve hot.

Serves 4
Preparation time 15 minutes
Cooking time 15 minutes

130
CALORIES
PER SERVING

Baked peaches

- **2 large, slightly underripe peaches, halved and pitted**
- **oil, for greasing**
- **a few saffron threads**
- **a few drops of almond extract**
- **½ cup crunchy oat cereal**
- **2 tablespoons orange juice**
- **2 inch cinnamon stick, broken into 8 pieces**

To serve
- **½ slightly underripe mango, thinly sliced**
- **1 teaspoon grated semisweet chocolate (optional)**

1 Scoop some of the flesh out of the peach halves and chop finely. Place the halved peaches, skin side down, in a lightly oiled baking dish.

2 Mix together the chopped peach flesh, saffron, almond extract, oat cereal, and orange juice in a bowl. Spoon the mixture carefully into the peach halves, then push the cinnamon stick pieces into the peaches.

3 Bake in a preheated oven, at 350°F, for 15 minutes. Serve each peach half with mango slices and a sprinkling of grated semisweet chocolate, if using.

197
CALORIES
PER SERVING

Serves 4
Preparation time 10 minutes
Cooking time 20 minutes

Blueberry & lemon pancakes

- 1 cup all-purpose flour
- 2 teaspoons baking powder
- finely grated rind of ½ lemon
- 1 tablespoon superfine or granulated sugar
- 1 egg, lightly beaten
- 1 tablespoon lemon juice
- ⅔ cup low-fat milk
- scant 1 cup (4 ounces) blueberries
- vegetable oil, for frying

1 Sift the flour and baking powder into a bowl and stir in the lemon rind and sugar. Add the egg and lemon juice and gradually beat in the milk to make a smooth, thick batter. Stir in the blueberries.

2 Heat a flat griddle pan or large, nonstick skillet and rub it with a sheet of paper towel drizzled with a little oil. Drop spoonfuls of the batter, spaced well apart, on the pan and cook for 2–3 minutes, until bubbles form on the surface and the underside is golden brown. Turn the pancakes over and cook on the other side. Wrap them in a dish towel and keep warm. Repeat with the remaining batter to make 8 pancakes. Serve warm.

Fruit salad with banana cream

- 1 ruby grapefruit
- 2 oranges
- 2 kiwis, peeled
- 1 ripe banana
- scant 1 cup low-fat fromage blanc or nonfat Greek yogurt
- 1 tablespoon honey

1 Cut the top and bottom off the grapefruit with a serrated knife to reveal the flesh, then cut away the remaining peel and pith. Holding the fruit above a serving bowl, cut between the membranes to release the fruit segments. Repeat the process with the oranges.

2 Cut the kiwis in half, then into thin wedges. Mix with the citrus fruit. Cover and chill.

3 When ready to serve, mash the banana with a fork and stir it into the fromage blanc with the honey. Spoon the fruit salad into 4 serving bowls and serve topped with the banana cream.

Serves 6
Preparation time 20 minutes, plus soaking, cooling and chilling
Cooking time 8–9 minutes

Rhubarb & ginger parfait

- 13 ounces trimmed blanched rhubarb
- 1 inch piece of fresh ginger root, peeled and finely chopped
- 1/3 cup water
- 3 teaspoons powdered gelatin
- 4 egg yolks
- 1/3 cup granulated sweetener
- scant 1 cup skim milk
- 2 egg whites
- 1/2 cup low-fat crème fraîche or nonfat Greek yogurt
- a few drops pink food coloring (optional)
- orange rind, to decorate

1 Slice the rhubarb and put the pieces in a saucepan with the ginger and 2 tablespoons of the measured water. Cover and simmer for 5 minutes, until just tender and still bright pink. Mash or puree.

2 Put the remaining water in a small bowl and sprinkle with the gelatin, making sure that all the powder is absorbed by the water. Set aside to soak for 5 minutes.

3 Whisk the egg yolks and sweetener until just mixed. Pour the milk into a small saucepan and bring just to a boil. Gradually whisk the milk into the egg yolks, then pour the mixture back into the saucepan. Slowly bring the custard almost to a boil, stirring continuously, until it coats the back of the spoon. Do not let the custard boil or the eggs will curdle.

4 Take the pan off the heat and stir in the gelatin until it has dissolved. Pour into a bowl, stir in the cooked rhubarb, and let cool.

5 Whisk the egg whites until stiff, moist peaks form. Fold the crème fraîche and a few drops of coloring, if used, into the cooled custard, then fold in the whisked whites. Spoon into 6 glasses and chill for 4 hours, until lightly set. Decorate with orange rind just before serving.

Serves 4
Preparation time 5 minutes
Cooking time 25 minutes

127
CALORIES
PER SERVING

Fruity baked apples

- **4 large sweet, crisp apples**
- **1 cup (4 ounces) dried fruit, such as cranberries, golden raisins, and chopped apricots**
- **4 teaspoons demerara or other raw sugar**

1 Core the apples and score a line around the middle of each and arrange them in an ovenproof dish. Stuff the cored center of the apples with the dried fruit.

2 Sprinkle with the sugar and bake in a preheated oven, at 400°F, for 25 minutes or until the apples are tender. Cut in half and serve.

Makes 12
Preparation time 10 minutes
Cooking time 10–12 minutes

Parmesan & herb biscuits

- 2 cups all-purpose flour, plus extra for dusting
- 2 teaspoons baking powder
- 6 tablespoons unsalted butter, diced
- ¼ cup grated Parmesan cheese
- 3 tablespoons chopped fresh mixed herbs, such as oregano and chives
- 1 egg, lightly beaten
- 2 tablespoons buttermilk

1 Sift the flour and baking powder into a large bowl, add the butter, and rub in with the fingertips until the mixture resembles fine bread crumbs. Add 3 tablespoons of the Parmesan and the herbs and stir together.

2 Beat together the egg and buttermilk in a small bowl. Use a knife or fork to combine the wet and dry ingredients lightly and bring them together to form a ball.

3 Shape the dough into a circle, about 1 inch thick and press out 12 circles with a 2 inch plain cutter. Place the circles on a lightly floured baking sheet and sprinkle with the reserved Parmesan.

4 Bake in a preheated oven, at 425°F, for 10–12 minutes, until golden and well risen. Serve warm. The biscuits can be stored in an airtight container for up to 3 days.

Makes 16
Preparation time 10 minutes
Cooking time 35 minutes

156
CALORIES
PER SERVING

Breakfast cereal bars

- 7 tablespoons butter, softened, plus extra for greasing
- 2 tablespoons packed light brown sugar
- 2 tablespoons light corn syrup
- 3 cups millet flakes
- ¼ cup quinoa
- ⅓ cup dried cherries or cranberries
- ½ cup golden raisins
- 3 tablespoons sunflower seeds
- 2 tablespoons sesame seeds
- 2½ tablespoons flaxseeds
- ½ cup plus 1 tablespoon unsweetened dry coconut
- 2 eggs, lightly beaten

1 Beat together the butter, sugar, and syrup in a large bowl until creamy. Add all the remaining ingredients and beat well until combined.

2 Turn the batter into a greased 11 × 8 inch shallow rectangular baking pan and level the surface with the back of a tablespoon.

3 Bake in a preheated oven, at 350°F, for 35 minutes, until deep golden. Let cool in the pan. Turn out onto a wooden board and carefully cut into 16 bars using a serrated knife. The bars can be stored in an airtight container for up to 5 days.

Makes 12
Preparation time 15 minutes
Cooking time 20–30 minutes

Apple & blackberry muffins

- ⅓ cup firmly packed light brown sugar
- 1 (5 ounces) red apple, cored and diced
- 1⅓ cups (7 ounces) coarsely chopped blackberries
- 1 teaspoon ground cinnamon
- 2 cups whole-wheat flour
- 4 teaspoons baking powder
- 2 eggs, beaten
- ½ cup low-fat milk
- ½ cup canola oil, plus extra for cooking

1 Mix together the sugar, apple, blackberries, and cinnamon in a bowl.

2 Sift the flour and baking powder into a separate bowl and make a well in the center. Mix together the eggs, milk, and oil in a small bowl, then pour into the well and stir until blended. Stir in the fruit mixture, being careful not to overmix. Divide the batter among the sections of a lightly oiled or paper liner-lined 12-cup muffin pan.

3 Bake in a preheated oven, at 400°F, for 20–30 minutes or until a toothpick inserted into the center comes out clean. Transfer the muffins to a wire rack to cool. The muffins can be stored in an airtight container for up to 3 days.

Makes 12 slices
Preparation time 15 minutes, plus cooling
Cooking time 15–20 minutes

122 CALORIES PER SERVING

Baked almond & apricot cake

- **4 eggs**
- **⅔ cup superfine or granulated sugar**
- **½ teaspoon almond extract**
- **⅓ cup all-purpose flour**
- **¾ cup ground almonds (almond meal)**
- **butter, for greasing**

Apricot filling
- **1 cup dried apricots**
- **⅔–1 cup water**
- **½ cup low-fat fromage blanc or nonfat Greek yogurt**

1 Put the eggs, sugar, and almond extract in a large bowl and beat until thick and frothy. Sift the flour into the bowl and gently fold in with the ground almonds.

2. Divide the cake batter between 2 lined and lightly greased 7 inch round cake pans. Bake in a preheated oven, at 350°F, for 15–20 minutes. Let cool in the pans for 10 minutes, then loosen the edges with a knife and turn out onto a wire rack to cool.

3 Meanwhile, make the filling, put the apricots in a small saucepan with the measured water, cover, and simmer for 10 minutes, until softened. Transfer to a blender or food processor and blend until smooth. Let cool, then sandwich the cake together with the apricot filling and the fromage frais.

Makes 8
Preparation time 10 minutes
Cooking time 18 minutes

CALORIES
PER SERVING

Rhubarb bars

- ¼ cup margarine
- 2 tablespoons light corn syrup
- 1 tablespoon packed light brown sugar
- ¾ cup plus 1 tablespoon rolled oats
- ⅔ cup whole-wheat flour, sifted
- pinch of ground ginger
- 3½ tablespoons chopped pecans
- ⅓ cup rhubarb compote or stewed rhubarb

1 Put the margarine, syrup, and sugar in a saucepan and heat gently until the sugar is dissolved. Stir in the oats, flour, ginger, and nuts and combine well.

2 Spoon two-thirds of the batter into a 6 inch square, nonstick baking pan and gently press down. Spoon the rhubarb over the batter, sprinkle with the remaining oat mixture, and press down lightly.

3 Bake in a preheated oven, at 350°F, for 15 minutes, until golden. Let cool in the pan, marking the cake into 8 rectangles while still warm.

300 CALORIES AND UNDER

288
CALORIES
PER SERVING

Serves 4
Preparation time 20 minutes
Cooking time 40–50 minutes

Spicy lentil & tomato soup

- 1 tablespoon vegetable oil
- 1 large onion, finely chopped
- 2 garlic cloves, finely chopped
- 1 small green chile, seeded and finely chopped
- 1¼ cups red lentils, washed and drained
- 1 bay leaf
- 3 celery sticks, thinly sliced
- 3 carrots, thinly sliced
- 1 leek, trimmed and thinly sliced
- 6⅓ cups vegetable stock
- 1⅔ cups canned diced tomatoes
- 2 tablespoons tomato paste
- ½ tablespoon ground turmeric
- ½ teaspoon ground ginger
- 1 tablespoon cilantro leaves
- ground black pepper

1 Heat the oil in a large saucepan, add the onion, garlic, and chile, and sauté gently for 4–5 minutes, until softened.

2 Add the lentils, bay leaf, celery, carrots, leek, and vegetable stock. Cover and bring to a boil, then reduce the heat and simmer for 30–40 minutes. Remove the bay leaf.

3 Stir in the tomatoes, tomato paste, turmeric, ginger, cilantro, and black pepper to taste. Let cool slightly, then transfer to a blender or food processor and blend until smooth, adding more stock or water, if necessary. Return to the pan and reheat gently before serving.

Serves 4
Preparation time 10 minutes
Cooking time 25–30 minutes

300
CALORIES
PER SERVING

Hearty seafood soup

- 1 tablespoon butter
- 1 onion, chopped
- 1 bay leaf
- 2 celery sticks, finely sliced
- 2–3 (10 ounces) red-skinned or white round potatoes, peeled and cubed
- 2 cups skim milk
- 2 cups fish stock
- 12 ounces mixed boneless, skinless fish fillets, such as cod and salmon, cubed
- 3½ ounces cooked, peeled shrimp
- ⅔ cup frozen peas
- ⅔ cup frozen corn kernels
- salt and ground black pepper

To garnish
- 3 tablespoons chopped parsley
- 2 tomatoes, finely chopped

1 Melt the butter in a large saucepan, add the onion, bay leaf, celery, and potatoes, and sauté for 3–4 minutes.

2 Add the milk and fish stock and bring to a boil, then reduce the heat, cover, and simmer for 15–20 minutes, until the potatoes are cooked.

3 Add the fish, shrimp, peas, and corn and simmer for another 5 minutes or until the fish is cooked through.

4 Season with salt and black pepper and serve sprinkled with the parsley and chopped tomatoes.

285
CALORIES
PER SERVING

Serves 6
Preparation time 10 minutes
Cooking time 8 minutes

Green bean & asparagus salad

- 2¼ cups (8 ounces) trimmed fine green beans
- 13 ounces asparagus, trimmed
- 6 eggs
- 5 cups (3½ ounces) arugula
- ¾ cup pitted ripe black olives
- 3 ounces Parmesan cheese shavings

Dressing
- ⅓ cup olive oil
- 1 tablespoon black olive pesto or tapenade
- 1 tablespoon balsamic vinegar
- salt and ground black pepper

1 Put the green beans in a steamer set over a saucepan of boiling water, cover, and cook for 3 minutes. Add the asparagus and cook for another 5 minutes, until the vegetables are just tender.

2 Meanwhile, put the eggs in a small saucepan, cover with cold water, and bring to a boil. Simmer for 6 minutes, until cooked but still soft in the center.

3 Make the dressing by combining the oil, pesto or tapenade, and vinegar in a small bowl with a little salt and black pepper.

4 Arrange the arugula in the center of 6 serving plates. Drain and rinse the eggs with cold water. Drain again, gently peel away the shells, and halve each egg. Place 2 halves on each mound of arugula. Arrange the beans and asparagus around the edge, then drizzle with the dressing. Add the olives and top with the Parmesan shavings. Serve immediately.

Serves 4
Preparation time 15 minutes
Cooking time 2½ minutes

300
CALORIES
PER SERVING

Warm scallop salad with strawberry dressing

- **12 large scallops, without corals, each cut into 3 slices**
- **juice of 1 lemon**
- **8 cups (8 ounces) mixed salad greens**
- **20 wild strawberries or 8 larger strawberries, hulled and sliced, to garnish**
- **salt and ground black pepper**

Dressing
- **about 1¾ cups (8 ounces) hulled wild strawberries**
- **2 tablespoons balsamic vinegar**
- **1 tablespoon lemon juice**
- **¼ cup olive oil**

Leek garnish
- **1 tablespoon olive oil**
- **3 leeks, trimmed and cut into matchstick strips**

1 Place the dressing ingredients in a blender or food processor and blend until smooth. Pass the puree through a fine strainer or cheesecloth to remove the seeds and set aside.

2 Season the scallops with salt, black pepper, and the lemon juice.

3 To make the garnish, heat the oil in a nonstick skillet over high heat, add the leeks, and sauté for 1 minute or until golden brown. Remove from the skillet and set aside. In the same skillet, cook the scallop slices for 20–30 seconds on each side.

4 Divide the salad greens evenly among 4 serving plates. Arrange the scallop slices over the salad.

5 In a small saucepan, gently heat the strawberry dressing for 20–30 seconds, then pour it over the scallops and salad greens. Sprinkle with the leek garnish and sliced strawberries. Sprinkle with a little black pepper and serve.

Serves 4
Preparation time 30 minutes
Cooking time 13 minutes

Thai mussel curry with ginger

- ½–1 large red chile, to taste
- 2 shallots, quartered
- 1 lemon grass stem
- 1 inch piece of fresh ginger root, peeled and chopped
- 1 tablespoon sunflower oil
- 1⅔ cups can reduced-fat coconut milk
- 4–5 kaffir lime leaves
- ⅔ cup fish stock
- 2 teaspoons Thai fish sauce
- 3 pounds fresh mussels, soaked in cold water
- small bunch of cilantro, torn into pieces, to garnish

1 Halve the chile and keep the seeds for extra heat, if desired. Put the chile, shallots, and lemon grass into a food processor with the ginger and process together until finely chopped.

2 Heat the oil in large, deep saucepan, add the finely chopped ingredients, and cook over medium heat for 5 minutes, stirring until softened. Add the coconut milk, kaffir lime leaves, fish stock, and fish sauce and cook for 3 minutes. Set aside until ready to finish.

3 Meanwhile, pick over the mussels and discard any that are opened or have cracked shells. Scrub with a small nailbrush, remove any barnacles, and pull off the small, hairy beards. Put them in a bowl of clean water and let stand until ready to cook.

4 Reheat the coconut milk mixture. Drain the mussels and add to the mixture. Cover the pan with a lid and cook for about 5 minutes, until the mussel shells have opened.

5 Spoon the mussels and the coconut sauce into bowls, discarding any mussels that have not opened. Garnish with the cilantro.

Serves 6
Preparation time 20 minutes
Cooking time 15 minutes

229
CALORIES
PER SERVING

Smoked salmon, ricotta & artichoke crepes

- ¾ cup buckwheat flour
- 1 egg
- 1 cup low-fat milk
- 2 tablespoons sunflower oil
- 8 ounces smoked salmon, sliced
- 13 ounces canned artichoke hearts, drained and quartered
- juice of 1 lemon
- salt and ground black pepper

Ricotta filling
- ½ cup ricotta cheese
- 3 tablespoons chopped parsley or mixed parsley and basil, plus extra to garnish
- 1 small garlic clove, crushed (optional)
- grated rind of ½ lemon

1 Put the flour, egg, a little of the milk, and some salt in a bowl and whisk until smooth. Gradually whisk in the remaining milk to make a batter.

2 To make the filling, mix together the ricotta, herbs, garlic, if using, and lemon rind in a bowl and season lightly. Set aside.

3 Heat a little of the oil in a nonstick skillet. When it is hot, pour the excess into a small, heatproof bowl. Drizzle in 3 tablespoons of the batter to make a lacy thin pancake, or crepe, about 7 inches in diameter and cook until the underside is browned. Loosen with a spatula, turn over the crepe, and cook on the other side. Transfer to a serving plate and keep warm. Repeat with the remaining mixture to make 6 crepes, adding more oil, if necessary.

4 Place each crepe on a serving plate, divide the ricotta filling among them, and top with strips of smoked salmon and artichoke quarters. Drizzle with lemon juice and sprinkle with black pepper. Fold the crepes over the filling and serve garnished with some extra chopped herbs.

Serves 4
Preparation time 15 minutes
Cooking time 20 minutes

Cod with spicy lima beans & tomatoes

- 2 teaspoons vegetable oil
- 1 celery stick, finely diced
- 1 onion, finely chopped
- 1 garlic clove, crushed, or 1 teaspoon minced garlic
- 1⅔ cups canned crushed tomatoes, undrained
- 2 tablespoons tomato paste
- 2 cups rinsed and drained canned lima beans
- 1 green chile, seeded and finely chopped
- ½ cup dry white wine
- 1 pound cod fillet or any boneless white fish fillets, cut into cubes
- ground black pepper
- 2 tablespoons chopped parsley, to garnish

1 Heat the oil in a nonstick saucepan, add the celery, onion, and garlic, and cook for about 5 minutes, until softened. Add the tomatoes, tomato paste, beans, and chile and simmer, uncovered, for 10 minutes.

2 Meanwhile, heat the wine in a separate saucepan. Add the fish and poach gently for about 3–4 minutes, until just cooked through.

3 Combine the fish and its cooking liquid with the bean and tomato mixture and heat through. Season with black pepper and serve garnished with parsley.

Serves 4
Preparation time 30 minutes
Cooking time 8 minutes

234
CALORIES
PER SERVING

Flounder packages with orange & radicchio salad

- 1 (11½ ounces) fennel bulb, trimmed and finely chopped
- 2 red chiles, seeded and chopped
- ¼ cup lemon juice
- 2 teaspoons olive oil
- 4 flounder fillets, about 1 pound 6 ounces in total
- small handful of dill, chopped
- ½ lemon, cut into wedges, to serve

Orange and radicchio salad
- 2 large oranges
- 2 small heads (7 ounces) red radicchio, leaves separated

1 Mix together the fennel, chiles, lemon juice, and oil in a nonmetallic bowl and set aside.

2 Cut 4 sheets of nonstick parchment paper, each 14 × 7 inches, and fold them in half widthwise. Lay ½ sheet over a plate and arrange a fish fillet on one side of the fold. Sprinkle with some chopped dill and fold over the paper to enclose the filling. Fold in the edges and pleat to secure. Repeat with the remaining fish.

3 Place the wrapped fish on a baking sheet and bake in a preheated oven, at 425°F, for about 8 minutes or until the paper is puffed up and brown.

4 Meanwhile, make the salad. Cut the top and bottom off the oranges with a serrated knife to reveal the flesh, then cut away the remaining peel and pith. Holding the fruit above a serving bowl, cut between the membranes to release the fruit segments. Add the radicchio and gently toss together.

5 Place each fish package on a large plate and cut an X shape slit in the top and curl back the paper, or pull the paper apart to open the package, releasing a fragrant puff of steam. Serve with bowls of the fennel mixture, the orange-and-radicchio salad, and lemon wedges.

Serves 6
Preparation time 15 minutes
Cooking time 12–13 minutes

Broiled sea bass with cherry tomatoes

- 1 tablespoon olive oil
- 1 onion, finely chopped
- 18 (10 ounces) cherry tomatoes, halved
- 2 large pinches of saffron threads (optional)
- ⅔ cup dry white wine
- ½ cup fish stock
- grated rind of 1 lemon, the rest halved and thinly sliced
- 12 small sea bass fillets, about 3½ ounces each, rinsed in cold water
- 1 teaspoon fennel seeds
- salt and ground black pepper
- basil or oregano leaves, to garnish (optional)

1 Heat the oil in a skillet, add the onion, and sauté for 5 minutes, until softened and lightly browned. Add the tomatoes, saffron, if using, wine, and stock and stir in the lemon rind and a little salt and black pepper. Bring to a boil and cook for 2 minutes.

2 Pour the mixture into the bottom of an aluminum foil-lined broiler pan, add the lemon slices, and set aside until ready to cook.

3 Arrange the fish fillets, skin side up, on top of the tomato mixture. Use a teaspoon to scoop some of the juices over the skin, then sprinkle with salt and black pepper and the fennel seeds.

4 Cook under a preheated broiler for 5–6 minutes, until the skin is crispy and the fish flakes easily when pressed with a knife. Serve sprinkled with basil or oregano leaves, if desired.

Serves 4
Preparation time 15 minutes
Cooking time 15 minutes

300
CALORIES
PER SERVING

Honey-glazed tuna

- **4 tuna steaks, about 4 ounces each**
- **2 teaspoons olive oil**

Glaze
- **1 tablespoon honey**
- **2 tablespoons whole-grain mustard**
- **1 teaspoon tomato paste**
- **2 tablespoons orange juice**
- **1 tablespoon red wine vinegar or balsamic vinegar**
- **ground black pepper**

Parsnip puree
- **1 parsnip, cut into chunks**
- **2 potatoes, cut into chunks**
- **¼ cup plain yogurt**
- **2 teaspoons horseradish sauce (optional)**

1 Put all the ingredients for the glaze in a small saucepan and bring to a boil, then reduce the heat and simmer until the mixture reduces and is of a glaze consistency. Keep hot.

2 Make the parsnip puree. Steam the parsnip and potatoes until tender. Drain, if necessary, and place in a food processor or blender with the yogurt, horseradish sauce, if using, and black pepper to taste. Process until blended. Keep warm or reheat prior to serving.

3 Brush the tuna with the oil. Cook in a preheated, hot ridged grill pan or skillet, on a barbecue grill, or or under a broiler for 1–2 minutes. Turn the tuna over and spoon the glaze over the top. Cook for another 1–2 minutes, until still moist and slightly pink in the center.

4 Spoon a mound of the parsnip puree onto 4 serving plates and top each with a tuna steak. Serve with any remaining glaze spooned over the top.

Serves 4
Preparation time 5 minutes
Cooking time 25 minutes

Steamed fish with ginger & coconut milk

- 1½ pounds fish fillets, such as salmon, cod, or red snapper, skinned
- ½ teaspoon salt
- 2 tablespoons vegetable oil
- 3 garlic cloves, finely sliced
- 1 cup finely sliced onion
- 1½ tablespoons oyster sauce
- ⅓ cup coconut milk
- 1 inch cube fresh ginger root, peeled and finely sliced into slivers
- 2 scallions, finely sliced
- 4 medium mushrooms, finely sliced
- ¼–⅓ cup roasted peanuts
- ground black pepper

1 Wash the fish and pat it dry. Put the fish onto a heatproof dish or plate that will fit into your steamer or on a rack in a saucepan. Rub the fish with the salt and season with black pepper.

2 Place a strainer over a bowl and cover a plate in paper towels. Heat the oil in a skillet over medium-low heat. When the oil is hot, put in the garlic slivers and sauté until golden. Remove with a slotted spoon and place in the strainer, then transfer to the paper towels. Repeat with the onion slices.

3 Combine the oyster sauce with 2 tablespoons of the coconut milk and spread the mixture evenly over the fish. Sprinkle the ginger, scallions, mushrooms, fried garlic, and half the fried onions over the top.

4 Place the plate with the fish on the rack in the steamer and cover. Build up steam over high heat for 2 minutes, then turn down the heat to medium-high and steam the fish for another 18 minutes.

5 Carefully lift the plate from the steamer. Transfer some of the sauce around the fish to a small saucepan, add the rest of the coconut milk, and heat gently. Pour the sauce over the fish and sprinkle with the remaining onions and the peanuts. Serve immediately.

Serves 4
Preparation time 10 minutes
Cooking time 18 minutes

203
CALORIES
PER SERVING

Shrimp & cucumber curry

- 1 cup finely chopped onion
- 4 garlic cloves, finely chopped
- 2 tablespoons ground coriander
- 1 tablespoon ground fennel
- 1 teaspoon ground white pepper
- 1 tablespoon ground cumin
- 1 teaspoon ground turmeric
- 2 cups water
- 3–4 dried hot chiles
- 1 (10 ounces) cucumber, peeled and thickly sliced
- 12 ounces raw shrimp, peeled and deveined
- ¾ teaspoon salt
- ¾ teaspoon sugar
- 1⅔ cups canned coconut milk

Garlic garnish
- 2 tablespoons vegetable oil
- 2 garlic cloves, finely sliced
- ¼ cup finely sliced onion
- 1 teaspoon whole fennel seeds

1 Mix together the chopped onions, chopped garlic, ground coriander, ground fennel, white pepper, cumin, turmeric, and measured water in a medium saucepan. Crumble in the red chiles, then stir thoroughly. Bring to a boil and boil, uncovered, for 5 minutes.

2 Add the cucumber and simmer for 5 minutes, then add the shrimp, salt, and sugar. Reduce the heat and simmer for another 1 minute, until the shrimp turn pink.

3 Add the coconut milk and return to a boil, then reduce the heat and simmer for 1 minute, stirring continuously. Remove the pan from the heat.

4 To make the garlic garnish, heat the oil in a small skillet, add the sliced garlic and onions, and cook until golden. Add the fennel seeds, stir once, and then pour the garlic mixture into the pan containing the curry. Cover immediately to seal the aromas and serve.

Serves 4
Preparation time 20 minutes
Cooking time 40–45 minutes

Thai coconut chicken

- **4 boneless, skinless chicken breasts, about 4 ounces each, cut into small pieces**
- **1 tablespoon refined peanut oil**
- **2 cups chicken stock**
- **1²/₃ cups canned coconut milk**
- **salt and ground black pepper**
- **coarsely chopped cilantro, to garnish**

Curry paste

- **1 green chile, seeded and coarsely chopped**
- **1 small onion, coarsely chopped**
- **3 garlic cloves, chopped**
- **3 cups (2 ounces) fresh cilantro**
- **2 teaspoons Thai fish sauce**
- **¼ teaspoon ground turmeric**
- **1 lemon grass stalk, coarsely chopped**
- **grated rind and juice of 1 lime**
- **2 teaspoons superfine or granulated sugar**
- **2½ tablespoons peeled and coarsely chopped fresh ginger root**

1 To make the curry paste, place all the paste ingredients in a food processor or blender and blend until smooth, scraping the mixture down from the sides of the bowl when necessary.

2 Season the chicken lightly with salt and black pepper. Heat the oil in a large saucepan, add the chicken, and cook gently for 5 minutes.

3 Meanwhile, put the stock and curry paste in a saucepan and bring to a boil. Cook, uncovered, for 15–20 minutes, until most of the liquid has evaporated.

4 Add the chicken and coconut milk to the curry mixture and cook for about 20 minutes, until the chicken is very tender. Serve garnished with chopped cilantro.

Serves 4
Preparation time 10 minutes, plus marinating
Cooking time 30 minutes

300
CALORIES
PER SERVING

Chicken breasts with soy glaze

- 4 chicken breasts, about 4 ounces each
- ¼ cup dark soy sauce
- 2 tablespoons packed light brown sugar
- 2 garlic cloves, crushed
- 2 tablespoons white wine vinegar
- ½ cup freshly squeezed orange juice
- ground black pepper

1 Lay the chicken breasts on a cutting board and slice each in half horizontally. Place in a large, shallow ovenproof dish, in which the breasts fit snugly.

2 Mix together the soy sauce, sugar, garlic, vinegar, orange juice, and black pepper and pour the mixture over the chicken. Cover and let marinate in the refrigerator until ready to cook.

3 Bake in a preheated oven, at 350°F, for 30 minutes, until the chicken is cooked through. Serve the chicken with the cooking juices spooned over the top.

275
CALORIES
PER SERVING

Serves 4
Preparation time 10 minutes
Cooking time 35–45 minutes

Baked herbed chicken & vegetables

- 1 pound new potatoes
- 4 chicken breasts, about 4 ounces each
- ⅓ cup fresh mixed herbs, such as parsley, chives, chervil, and mint
- 1 garlic clove, crushed
- ⅓ cup crème fraîche or fat-free sour cream
- 8 baby leeks
- 2 heads of endive, halved lengthwise
- ⅔ cup chicken stock
- ground black pepper

1 Cook the potatoes in a saucepan of boiling water for 12–15 minutes, until tender. Drain, then cut into bite-size pieces.

2 Make a slit lengthwise down the side of each chicken breast to form a pocket, making sure that you do not cut all the way through. Mix together the herbs, garlic, and crème fraîche, season well with black pepper, then spoon a little into each chicken pocket.

3 Place the leeks, endive, and potatoes in an ovenproof dish. Pour the stock over the vegetables, then lay the chicken breasts on top. Spoon the remaining crème fraîche mixture over the top.

4 Bake in a preheated oven, at 400°F, for 25–30 minutes, until the chicken is cooked through and the vegetables are tender. Serve hot.

Serves 4
Preparation time 10 minutes
Cooking time 11–12 minutes

227
CALORIES
PER SERVING

Easy corned beef hash

- 1 teaspoon vegetable oil
- 1 onion, coarsely chopped
- 4 cups (11½ ounces) coarsely chopped cooked new potatoes
- 10 ounces corned beef, coarsely chopped
- 1 tablespoon chopped parsley
- Worcestershire sauce, to taste
- ground black pepper

1 Heat the oil in a large, nonstick skillet, add the onion, and sauté for 5 minutes, until softened. Add the potatoes and corned beef and cook for another 6–7 minutes, turning the mixture occasionally so that parts of it become crisp.

2 Add the parsley and stir through the mixture, season to taste with Worcestershire sauce and black pepper, and serve immediately.

Top tip

It takes 20 minutes for your brain to register that your stomach is full, so eating slowly is a great trick to stop you from overeating on your "off" days.

Serves 4
Preparation time 15 minutes
Cooking time 11–12 minutes

Tamarind & lemon grass beef

- 1 tablespoon olive oil
- 1 pound lean beef, cut into strips
- 2 lemon grass stalks, chopped
- 6 shallots, chopped
- 2 green chiles, chopped
- 3 tablespoons tamarind paste
- 2 tablespoons lime juice
- 2 teaspoons Thai fish sauce
- 2 teaspoons packed brown sugar
- 1 small (7 ounces) green papaya, shredded

1 Heat the oil in a wok or skillet over high heat, add the beef, and stir-fry for 2–3 minutes.

2 Add the lemon grass, shallots, and chiles, and stir-fry for another 5 minutes or until the meat is well browned.

3 Add the tamarind paste, lime juice, fish sauce, sugar, and green papaya and stir-fry for another 4 minutes. Serve immediately.

Top tip

If hunger is getting the better of you, try taking a brisk walk around the block or running up and down the stairs five times—anything to take your mind of that grumbling stomach.

Serves 4
Preparation time 10 minutes
Cooking time 7–8 minutes

290 CALORIES PER SERVING

Seared steak with Parmesan & arugula

- 3 tablespoons light olive oil
- 2 red onions, thickly sliced
- 1 pound tenderloin steak, cut into 8 steaks
- 9 cups (5 ounces) arugula
- 4 ounces Parmesan cheese shavings
- 3 tablespoons flat-leaf parsley
- 2 tablespoons balsamic vinegar
- ground black pepper

1 Heat 1 tablespoon of the oil in a skillet over medium heat, add the onions, and sauté for 5 minutes or until golden. Remove the onions from the pan and keep warm.

2 Increase the heat to high and add the steaks to the skillet. Cook for about ½–1 minute on each side or until sealed and seared.

3 Toss together the arugula, Parmesan shavings, parsley, balsamic vinegar, black pepper, and the remaining oil in a bowl.

4 Place a steak on each of 4 serving plates, add some of the salad mixture, and then another steak. Serve topped with the fried onions.

Serves 4
Preparation time 25 minutes, plus chilling
Cooking time 35–40 minutes

Kofta curry

- 1 small onion, chopped
- 2 teaspoons peeled and grated fresh ginger root
- 3 garlic cloves, coarsely chopped
- 3 tablespoons cilantro leaves
- 11 ounces lean ground lamb or beef
- ½ teaspoon chili powder
- ¼ teaspoon garam masala
- 1 tablespoon cornstarch

Sauce
- 1 tablespoon vegetable oil
- 1 small onion, finely chopped
- ¼ teaspoon cumin seeds
- 2–3 green cardamom pods
- 1 teaspoon ginger paste
- 1 teaspoon garlic paste
- ½ teaspoon chili powder
- ¼ teaspoon ground turmeric
- ¼ teaspoon garam masala
- ½ cup chopped tomato
- 1 tablespoon plain yogurt
- 2 cups water
- 1 green chile, seeded and finely chopped
- 2 tablespoons cilantro leaves

1 To make the koftas, place the onion, ginger, garlic, and cilantro in a food processor or blender and process until blended. Put the meat in a bowl and add the blended mixture, spices, and cornstarch, then knead until mixed. Cover and chill for 10–15 minutes to let the flavors develop.

2 To make the sauce, heat the oil in a heavy saucepan, add the onion, and sauté gently for 5 minutes. Add the cumin and cardamom and cook for about 2 minutes, until the onions are browned, then add the garlic and ginger paste and remaining spices. Cook for about 5 minutes, until the spices darken, adding a little water when necessary. Add the tomato and yogurt, stirring continuously.

3 Meanwhile, divide the kofta mixture into 16 equal portions and roll each portion into a smooth round ball. Cook the koftas under a preheated medium broiler for 10 minutes, turning once to drain off all the excess fat.

4 Add the koftas to the sauce mixture. Cook, stirring, for about 2 minutes, then add the measured water, cover, and simmer for 20–25 minutes. Stir in the chile and cilantro, adding a little boiling water, if necessary. Serve hot.

Serves 4
Preparation time 10 minutes, plus marinating
Cooking time 10–12 minutes

261 CALORIES PER SERVING

Pan-fried spiced lamb & beans

- ½ teaspoon ground cumin
- ½ teaspoon ground coriander
- pinch of chili powder
- 1 tablespoon olive oil
- 4 lean lamb cutlets
- 1 onion, sliced
- 1 garlic clove, crushed
- ¼ cup lemon juice
- 2½ cups rinsed and drained canned great Northern beans
- 1 tablespoon chopped mint
- 2 tablespoons low-fat crème fraîche or nonfat Greek yogurt

1 Mix together the cumin, coriander, chili powder, and half the oil in a nonmetallic bowl. Add the lamb, coat it in the spices, and let marinate for 10 minutes.

2 Heat the remaining oil in a nonstick skillet, add the onion and garlic, and sauté for 3–4 minutes, until softened.

3 Add the lamb and the marinade and cook the cutlets for 2–3 minutes on each side or until cooked to your liking.

4 Add the lemon juice, great Northern beans, mint, and crème fraîche and simmer for 1 minute, until warmed through. Serve immediately.

Serves 4
Preparation time 10 minutes, plus marinating
Cooking time 2–2½ hours

Lamb shanks with spiced beans & balsamic onions

- **4 lamb shanks, about 2½ pounds in total, fat removed**
- **4–5 rosemary sprigs**
- **2 garlic cloves, thinly sliced**
- **4 small red onions, halved**
- **3 tablespoons balsamic vinegar**

Marinade
- **small bunch of thyme, leaves removed from stems**
- **3 whole cardamom pods**
- **1 bay leaf**
- **pinch of saffron threads**
- **¼ cup lemon juice**
- **salt and ground black pepper**

Spiced beans
- **2 teaspoons canola oil**
- **½ teaspoon black mustard seeds**
- **½ teaspoon onion seeds**
- **1 tablespoon tomato paste**
- **pinch of ground turmeric**
- **¼–½ teaspoon chill powder**
- **3½ rinsed and drained canned pinto beans**
- **2 tablespoons chopped cilantro leaves, plus extra to garnish**

1 Place the shanks in a ceramic roasting pan, make slits in each shank, and push in sprigs of rosemary and slices of garlic.

2 Mix together the marinade ingredients in a nonmetallic bowl. Coat the lamb shanks, cover with aluminum foil, and let marinate in the refrigerator for at least 1 hour.

3 Cook the lamb in a preheated oven, at 325°F, for 2–2½ hours, basting every 45 minutes or so, until the meat is tender.

4 Meanwhile, place the halved onions, cut sides up, in a heatproof dish, pour the vinegar over them, and cook under a preheated medium broiler for about 20 minutes, until soft.

5 Prepare the beans. Heat the oil in a skillet, add the mustard and onion seeds, and cook over a low heat, letting them pop for a few seconds. Stir in the tomato paste, turmeric, and chili powder. Add the beans and a few tablespoons of hot water. Cover and cook for a few minutes. Stir in the cilantro and remove from the heat.

6 Serve the lamb with the spiced beans and broiled red onions, sprinkled with chopped cilantro.

Serves 4
Preparation time 10 minutes
Cooking time 12–14 minutes

280
CALORIES
PER SERVING

Lamb cutlets with herbed crust

- **12 lean lamb cutlets, about 1½ ounces each**
- **2 tablespoons pesto**
- **3 tablespoons multigrain bread crumbs**
- **1 tablespoon chopped walnuts, toasted**
- **1 teaspoon vegetable oil**
- **2 garlic cloves, crushed**
- **1¼ pounds greens of your choice, finely shredded and blanched**

1 Heat a nonstick skillet until hot, add the lamb cutlets, and cook for 1 minute on each side, then transfer to a baking sheet.

2 Mix together the pesto, bread crumbs, and walnuts in a bowl. Spoon the mixture on to one side of the cutlets, pressing down lightly. Place in a preheated oven, at 400°F, for 10–12 minutes.

3 Meanwhile, heat the oil in a skillet or wok, add the garlic, and stir-fry for 1 minute, then add the greens and stir-fry for another 3–4 minutes, until tender. Serve the lamb with the greens.

Serves 4
Preparation time 10 minutes, plus marinating
Cooking time 20 minutes

Marinated pork tenderloin

- **2 pork tenderloins, about 8 ounces each**
- **1 tablespoon flaxseeds**
- **⅔ cup dry white wine**

Marinade
- **1 cinnamon stick**
- **2 tablespoons soy sauce**
- **2 garlic cloves, crushed**
- **1 teaspoon peeled and grated fresh ginger root**
- **1 tablespoon honey**
- **1 teaspoon crushed coriander seeds**
- **1 teaspoon sesame oil**

1 Mix together the marinade ingredients, then place the pork tenderloins in a shallow nonmetallic dish and cover evenly with the marinade. Cover and let marinate in the refrigerator for at least 2–3 hours or preferably overnight.

2 When ready to cook, drain the pork, reserving the marinade. Lay the meat in the flaxseeds on both sides so it is evenly covered. Place on a baking sheet or in a roasting pan and seal it over high heat on the stove, then roast in a preheated oven, at 350°F, for 18–20 minutes or until golden brown.

3 Meanwhile, remove the cinnamon stick from the marinade and pour the liquid into a nonstick saucepan. Add the white wine and bring to a boil. Reduce the heat and simmer until it has the consistency of a sticky glaze. Remove from the heat and set aside.

4 Remove the pork from the oven and cut into ¼ inch slices. Serve drizzled with the glaze.

Serves 4
Preparation time 15 minutes
Cooking time 16 minutes

271
CALORIES
PER SERVING

Wild venison steaks with ratatouille

- 4 venison steaks, about 4 ounces each
- 2 tablespoons olive oil
- 1 garlic clove, crushed
- 1 red onion, chopped
- 4 scallions, sliced
- 1 yellow or red bell pepper, cored, seeded and chopped
- 2 small zucchini, finely sliced
- 1 small eggplant, cut into 1 inch cubes
- 6 small firm tomatoes, chopped
- ¼ cup chopped walnuts or almonds
- 2 tablespoons balsamic vinegar
- salt and ground black pepper
- chopped flat-leaf parsley, to garnish

1 Sandwich the venison steaks between sheets of wax paper, then roll with a rolling pin to flatten them. Season with salt and black pepper and rub in 1 tablespoon of the oil.

2 Heat the remaining oil in a deep skillet, add the garlic, red onion, and scallions, and stir-fry over medium-high heat for 2 minutes. Add the remaining ingredients, except the venison, and cook over medium heat for about 14 minutes, until the vegetables are tender.

3 Meanwhile, cook the steaks under a preheated broiler for 3–5 minutes on each side or until cooked to your liking. Wrap each steak in aluminum foil and let rest for 2–4 minutes.

4 Spoon a mound of the ratatouille onto 4 serving plates and top each with a steak. Serve garnished with chopped parsley.

Serves 4
Preparation time 15–20 minutes
Cooking time 25 minutes

Gado gado

- 1½ cups trimmed 2 inch green bean pieces
- 1½ cups cauliflower florets
- 3 cups broccoli florets
- 2 cups finely shredded cabbage
- 3 hard-boiled eggs, quartered
- 2 large tomatoes, quartered
- 1 large orange bell pepper, cored, seeded, and cut into thin slices
- ½ (5 ounces) cucumber, peeled and cut into chunky slices
- 1¼ cups bean sprouts
- salt

Peanut sauce
- 2 cups chicken or vegetable stock
- ½ cup chunky peanut butter
- 2 garlic cloves, finely chopped
- 1 scallion, finely chopped
- ½ teaspoon chili powder
- 1 tablespoon Thai fish sauce
- 5 teaspoons lime juice

1 Bring a medium saucepan of water to a boil, add a little salt, and keep at a gentle boil over medium-high heat. Add the green beans and boil for 3 minutes or until they are just tender. Remove with a slotted spoon, place in a colander, and refresh under cold running water. Place on a large serving plate.

2 Cook the cauliflower and broccoli for 2–3 minutes and refresh in the same way. Arrange in separate piles on the serving plate. Finally, cook the cabbage strips for 1 minute, drain, and refresh under cold water. Add to the plate.

3 Arrange the egg, tomatoes, bell pepper, cucumber, and bean sprouts on the plate. Cover with plastic wrap and set aside.

4 To make the sauce, heat the stock in a saucepan until nearly boiling. Remove from the heat. Put the peanut butter in a separate saucepan with the garlic, scallion, and chili powder. Gradually add the warm stock to the mixture, stirring continuously until thoroughly blended.

5 Add the fish sauce and lime juice to the sauce and bring to a boil. Reduce the heat to medium-low and simmer for 15 minutes, stirring occasionally, until thickened to a creamy consistency. Let cool slightly, then pour the warmed sauce over the vegetables and serve.

Serves 4
Preparation time 10 minutes
Cooking time 20–25 minutes

268
CALORIES
PER SERVING

Vegetable curry

- 1 tablespoon olive oil
- 1 onion, chopped
- 1 garlic clove, crushed
- 2 tablespoons medium curry paste
- 3 pounds prepared vegetables, such as zucchini, bell peppers, squash, mushrooms, and green beans
- ¾ cup canned diced tomatoes
- 1⅔ cups can reduced-fat coconut milk
- 2 tablespoons chopped cilantro

1 Heat the oil in a large saucepan, add the onion and garlic, and sauté for 2 minutes. Stir in the curry paste and sauté for another 1 minute.

2 Add the vegetables and cook for 2–3 minutes, stirring occasionally, then add the tomatoes and coconut milk. Stir well and bring to a boil, then reduce the heat and simmer for 12–15 minutes or until the vegetables are tender. Stir in the cilantro and serve.

Serves 4
Preparation time 20 minutes, plus marinating
Cooking time 40 minutes

Thai noodles with tofu

- 8 ounces tofu, diced
- 2 tablespoons dark soy sauce
- 1 teaspoon grated lime rind
- 6 ounces dried egg noodles
- 1¾ cups sliced button mushrooms
- 2 large carrots, cut into matchsticks
- 2 cups sugar snap peas
- 1⅓ cups shredded napa cabbage
- 2 tablespoons chopped cilantro

Broth
- 7½ cups vegetable stock
- 2 slices of fresh ginger root
- 2 garlic cloves
- 2 cilantro sprigs
- 2 lemon grass stalks, crushed
- 1 red chile, bruised

1 Mix together the tofu, soy sauce, and lime rind in a shallow nonmetallic dish. Let marinate for 30 minutes.

2 Meanwhile, make the broth. Put the vegetable stock in a large saucepan and add the ginger, garlic, cilantro sprigs, lemon grass, and chile. Bring to a boil, then reduce the heat, cover, and simmer for 30 minutes.

3 Strain the broth into another saucepan, return to a boil, and plunge in the noodles. Add the mushrooms and tofu with any remaining marinade. Reduce the heat and simmer gently for 4 minutes.

4 Stir in the carrots, sugar snap peas, cabbage, and chopped cilantro and cook for another 3–4 minutes. Serve immediately.

Serves 6
Preparation time 10 minutes
Cooking time 50 minutes

262
CALORIES
PER SERVING

Melanzane parmigiana

- 6 eggplants
- 1 tablespoon extra virgin olive oil
- 3⅓ cups canned diced tomatoes
- 2 garlic cloves, crushed
- 2 cups shredded cheddar cheese
- ½ cup fresh grated Parmesan cheese
- salt and ground black pepper

1 Trim the eggplants and cut lengthwise into thick slices. Brush them with the oil and put on 2 large baking sheets. Roast at the top of a preheated oven, at 400°F, for 10 minutes on each side, until golden and tender.

2 Meanwhile, put the tomatoes and garlic in a saucepan and bring to a boil. Reduce the heat and simmer for 10 minutes, then season with salt and black pepper.

3 Spoon a little of the tomato into an ovenproof dish and top with a layer of eggplants and some of the cheddar. Continue with the layers, finishing with a layer of cheddar on top. Sprinkle with the Parmesan and bake for 30 minutes, until the cheese is bubbling and golden. Serve hot.

Serves 2
Preparation time 5 minutes
Cooking time 10 minutes

Creamy mushrooms on toast

- 4 slices of whole-wheat bread
- 1 tablespoon avocado oil
- 1 tablespoon lime juice
- 1 small onion, chopped
- 8 mushrooms, sliced
- 1 tablespoon light soy sauce
- 2 tablespoons ricotta cheese

1 Place the bread on a baking sheet and bake in a preheated oven, at 350°F, for 5 minutes.

2 Meanwhile, heat the oil in a skillet, add the lime juice, onion, and mushrooms, and sauté until softened. Stir in the soy sauce and ricotta.

3 Pour the mixture on top of the toasted whole-wheat bread and serve.

Serves 4
Preparation time 20 minutes
Cooking time 25–30 minutes

293
CALORIES
PER SERVING

Artichoke pizza

- 12 inch store-bought pizza crust
- 6 canned artichoke hearts, drained
- handful of ripe black olives
- 6 strips of baked, smoked tofu
- 1 cup shredded reduced-fat Cheddar or other hard cheese (optional)

Tomato topping
- 1²/₃ cups canned tomatoes
- 1 onion, chopped
- 2 garlic cloves, chopped
- 1 teaspoon chopped oregano
- 1 green bell pepper, cored, seeded, and chopped
- 1 red bell pepper, cored, seeded, and chopped
- 1 carrot, shredded
- 1 tablespoon olive oil
- 1 tablespoon balsamic vinegar
- 6 mushrooms, sliced

1 To make the tomato topping, place the tomatoes in a blender or food processor and blend until smooth. Transfer to a large saucepan, add the onion, garlic, and oregano, and simmer gently for 20 minutes.

2 Stir the remaining topping ingredients into the pan, then pour the mixture over the pizza crust, spreading it right to the edges. Arrange the remaining ingredients and cheese, if using, on top.

3 Place the pizza on a baking sheet and bake in a preheated oven, at 400°F, for 5–10 minutes or until the cheese begins to bubble and turn brown. Cut into 4 and serve.

Serves 4
Preparation time 10 minutes
Cooking time 20 minutes

Wild mushroom omelets

- **2 tablespoons butter**
- **7 ounces wild mushrooms, trimmed and sliced**
- **8 extra-large eggs, beaten**
- **2 tablespoons chopped parsley**
- **½ cup shredded Gruyère cheese**
- **ground black pepper**

1 Melt a little of the butter in an omelet pan, add the mushrooms, and sauté for 5–6 minutes, until cooked and any moisture has evaporated. Remove the mushrooms from the pan.

2 Melt a little more butter in the same pan and add one-quarter of the beaten egg. Season well with black pepper and stir with a wooden spoon, bringing the cooked egg to the center of the pan and letting the runny egg flow to the edge of the pan and cook.

3 When there is only a little liquid egg left, sprinkle with a few mushrooms and some of the parsley and Gruyère. Fold the omelet over, tip onto a warm serving plate, and keep warm. Repeat with the remaining ingredients to make 4 omelets. Serve warm.

Serves 2
Preparation time 10 minutes
Cooking time 20–25 minutes

246
CALORIES
PER SERVING

Stuffed mushrooms

- 2 large, flat portobello mushrooms
- 2 tablespoons olive oil, plus extra for brushing
- 2 scallions, chopped
- ½ red bell pepper, cored, seeded, and chopped
- 1 small zucchini, chopped
- 4 pitted olives, chopped
- 2 tablespoons rolled oats
- 1 tablespoon chopped basil
- 1 tablespoon soy sauce
- 1 tablespoon lime juice
- salt and ground black pepper

1 Wipe the mushrooms clean with damp paper towels, then remove the stems, and chop them.

2 Heat the oil in a small saucepan, add the chopped mushroom stems, scallions, red bell pepper, zucchini, olives, and oats, and cook gently until the oats are golden. Stir in the basil, soy sauce, and lime juice.

3 Brush the mushroom caps with oil and place on a baking sheet. Spoon the oat mixture onto the mushrooms and season with salt and black pepper. Bake in a preheated oven, at 350°F, for 15–20 minutes, until the caps begin to soften, then serve.

Serves 6
Preparation time 5 minutes
Cooking time 30 minutes

Quick chickpea casserole

- ¼ cup olive oil
- 2 large onions, chopped
- 1–2 tablespoons ground cumin
- 4–5 garlic cloves, chopped
- 4¾ cups rinsed and drained canned chickpeas
- 1¼ cups vegetable stock
- juice of 1 lemon
- 1 pound fresh spinach leaves, coarsely chopped
- salt and ground black pepper

1 Heat the oil in a large saucepan, add the onions, and sauté over medium heat until softened. Add the cumin and garlic, stir, and cook for 1 minute.

2 Add the chickpeas, stock, and lemon juice, cover, and simmer for 20 minutes. Add the spinach and season with salt and black pepper. Mix well and cook for another 7 minutes.

3 Serve hot, at room temperature or cold. The flavor improves if the casserole is left overnight.

Serves 8
Preparation time 15 minutes
Cooking time 25–30 minutes

273
CALORIES
PER SERVING

Vegetable chili

- 3 tablespoons olive oil
- 3 onions, chopped
- 4 garlic cloves, chopped
- 1 large green bell pepper, cored, seeded, and chopped
- 1 large red bell pepper, cored, seeded, and chopped
- 2 tablespoons mild chili powder
- 2 tablespoons paprika
- 1 tablespoon ground cumin
- 1 bay leaf
- 2 teaspoons dried oregano
- 4 (1 pound) fresh tomatoes or 2 cups canned tomatoes, chopped
- 3 cups vegetable stock
- 2 cups rinsed and drained canned kidney or cranberry beans
- salt and ground black pepper

1 Heat the oil in a large saucepan, add the onions, garlic, and red and green bell peppers, and sauté over medium heat for 2–3 minutes. Add the chili powder, paprika, and cumin and cook for another 1 minute.

2 Add the remaining ingredients and bring to a boil, then reduce the heat and simmer for 20–25 minutes or until thickened. Season with salt and black pepper and serve.

296
CALORIES
PER SERVING

Serves 6
Preparation time 10 minutes
Cooking time 30 minutes

Potato & onion tortilla

- 6 (1½ pounds) baking potatoes
- ¼ cup olive oil
- 2 large onions, thinly sliced
- 6 eggs, beaten
- salt and ground black pepper

1 Slice the potatoes very thinly and toss them in a bowl with a little salt and black pepper. Heat the oil in a medium, heavy skillet, add the potatoes, and sauté very gently for 10 minutes, turning frequently, until softened but not browned.

2 Add the onions and sauté gently for another 5 minutes without browning. Spread the potatoes and onions in an even layer in the pan and reduce the heat as low as possible.

3 Pour in the eggs, cover, and cook very gently for about 15 minutes, until the eggs have set. (If the center of the omelett is too wet, place the pan under a preheated medium broiler to finish cooking.) Tip the tortilla onto a plate. Cut into 6 and serve warm or cold.

Serves 4
Preparation time 20 minutes
Cooking time 25–30 minutes

230
CALORIES
PER SERVING

Baked butternut squash
& goat cheese

- 6 (13 ounces) raw beets, peeled and diced
- 5 cups (1¼ pounds) peeled and seeded large butternut squash or pumpkin dice
- 1 red onion, cut into wedges
- 2 tablespoons olive oil
- 2 teaspoons fennel seeds
- 2 small goat cheeses, 3½ ounces each, halved
- salt and ground black pepper
- chopped rosemary, to garnish

1 Place the beets, squash, and onion in a roasting pan, drizzle with the oil, and sprinkle with the fennel seeds and salt and black pepper. Roast in a preheated oven, at 400°F, for 20–25 minutes, turning once, until well browned and tender.

2 Remove the pan from the oven and nestle the halves of goat cheese among the roasted vegetables. Sprinkle the cheese with a little salt and black pepper and drizzle with some of the pan juices.

3 Bake for about another 5 minutes, until the cheese is just beginning to melt. Sprinkle with rosemary and serve immediately.

230
CALORIES
PER SERVING

Serves 4
Preparation time 5 minutes, plus standing
Cooking time 25 minutes

Buckwheat pancakes

- 1/3 cup whole-wheat flour
- 1/3 cup buckwheat flour
- 1 egg
- 1 1/4 cups skim milk
- 8 teaspoons olive oil

1 Sift the flours into a bowl. Beat together the egg and milk, then slowly add to the flour. Stir until a smooth batter forms. Let stand for 20 minutes, then stir again.

2 Heat 1 teaspoon of the oil in a nonstick skillet. When hot, add 2 tablespoons of pancake batter. Cook for 2 minutes, until the underside is lightly browned, then turn the pancake over and cook on the other side. Transfer to a serving plate and keep warm. Repeat with the remaining batter to make 8 pancakes.

Serves 6
Preparation time 20 minutes
Cooking time 25–30 minutes

Apple & fig crisp

- 1 cup whole-wheat flour
- ¼ cup firmly packed brown sugar
- ¼ cup unsaturated spread
- 3 (1 pound) cooking apples, such as Granny Smiths, peeled, cored, and sliced
- 6 dried or fresh figs, diced
- grated rind and juice of 1 lemon
- 1 teaspoon ground cinnamon

1 Sift the flour into a large bowl, add the unsaturated spread, and lightly rub in with the fingertips until the mixture resembles coarse crumbs. Stir in the sugar.

2 Place the fruit in a 1¼ quart ovenproof dish. Add the lemon rind and juice and cinnamon. Spoon the crumb topping over the fruit and **b**ake in a preheated oven, at 350°F, for 25–30 minutes, until golden brown. Serve warm.

Top tip

The average food craving lasts about 10 minutes, so try to distract yourself to get past your hunger pang. Make yourself a cup of herbal tea, have a bath, or phone a friend.

Calorie counter

	Average portion	Calories
FRUIT		
Apples (weighed whole with core)		
Cox's Pippin	4½ ounces (about 1 medium)	53
Golden Delicious	4½ ounces (about 1 medium)	50
Granny Smith	4½ ounces (about 1 medium)	52
Apples (stewed with sugar)	3¾ ounces (about 1 medium)	81
Apricots (flesh only)	2¾ ounces (about 2 small)	25
Avocado (flesh only)	5 ounces (about 1 cup cubed)	266
Bananas	3½ ounces (about 1 small)	95
Blackberries	3½ ounces (about ⅔ cup)	25
Blueberries	1¾ ounces (about ⅓ cup)	35
Cherries (weighed with pits)	2¾ ounces (about ½ cup)	31
Clementines (weighed with peel and seeds)	2¾ ounces (about 1 medium)	22
Figs	2 ounces (about 1 large)	24
Fruit Salad	5 ounces (about ⅔ cup)	77
Grapefruit (weighed with peel and seeds)	6 ounces (about ¾ medium)	20
Grapes	3½ ounces (about ⅔ cup)	60
Kiwis (weighed with skin)	2⅔ ounces (about 1 medium)	32
Lemon, unpeeled	2 ounces (about ½ medium)	8
Lime, unpeeled	1½ ounces (about ½ medium)	4
Mango (weighed with skin and pit)	7 ounces (about 1 medium)	135
Melon (weighed with skin)		
Cantaloupe	6⅓ ounces (about 1 cup)	23
Galia	7 ounces (about 1¼ cups)	30
Honeydew	7 ounces (about 1¼ cups)	38
Nectarines (weighed with skin)	5¼ ounces (about 1 large)	54
Oranges (weighed with skin)	7 ounces (about 1 large)	52
Papaya (flesh only)	5¼ ounces (about 1 cup diced)	50
Peaches (weighed with pit)	5¼ ounces (about 1 large)	45
Pears (weighed whole with core)	5¼ ounces (about 1 small)	54
Pineapple	2¾ ounces (about ½ cup diced)	33
Plums (weighed with pit)	2½ ounces (about 1 medium)	24
Raspberries	2 ounces (about ½ cup)	15
Satsumas/Mandarin Oranges (weighed with skin)	3 ounces (1 small)	23
Strawberries	3½ ounces (about ⅔ cup hulled and halved)	27
Watermelon (flesh only)	7 ounces (about 1⅓ cups diced)	62
DRIED FRUIT, NUTS, AND SEEDS		
Almonds	½ ounce (about 2 tablespoons)	91
Apricots, dried	1 ounce (about 8 halves)	60
Brazil Nuts	⅓ ounce (about 2)	68
Cashew Nuts	⅓ ounce (about 1 tablespoon)	63
Cashew Nuts, roasted and salted	1 ounce (about 3½ tablespoons)	153
Chestnuts	1¾ ounces (about 4)	85
Cranberries, dried, sweetened	1 ounce (about 3 tablespoons)	82
Dates, dried, pitted	1¾ ounces (about 2 medium)	35
Figs, dried	¾ ounce (about 2 medium)	68
Hazelnuts	½ ounce (about 1 tablespoon)	65
Mixed Nuts	1½ ounces (about ⅓ cup)	243
Mixed Nuts and Raisins	1½ ounces (about ⅓ cup)	192
Peanuts, plain	½ ounce (about 1 tablespoon)	73
Peanuts, dry-roasted	1½ ounces (about ⅓ cup)	236
Pecans	¾ cup (about 3 tablespoons)	138
Pine Nuts	⅛ ounce (about ½ tablespoon)	34
Pistachio Nuts, roasted and salted	½ ounce (about 1 tablespoon)	60
Prunes, dried	2¼ ounces (about ½ cup)	93
Pumpkin Seeds	½ ounce (about 4 teaspoons)	91
Raisins, Golden	1 ounce (about 3 tablespoons)	73
Raisins, seedless	1 ounce (about 3 tablespoons)	76
Sunflower Seeds	½ ounce (about 5 teaspoons)	96
Walnuts	¾ ounce (about 3 tablespoons)	138

	Average portion	Calories

VEGETABLES (RAW, PREPARED, UNLESS OTHERWISE STATED)

	Average portion	Calories
Asparagus	4½ ounces (about 8 spears)	33
Beans		
Fava	4¼ ounces (about ¾ cup shelled)	58
Green	3 ounces (about ¾ cup pieces)	20
Runner	3 ounces (about ¾ cup pieces)	16
Beets	1½ ounces (about ½ medium)	18
Bell Peppers		
Green	5⅔ ounces (about 1 large)	24
Red	5⅔ ounces (about 1 large)	51
Yellow	5⅔ ounces (about 1 large)	42
Broccoli	3 ounces (about 1 cup florets)	20
Brussels Sprouts	3 ounces (about 5)	32
Cabbage		
Red	3 ounces (about 1 cup)	14
Savoy	3⅓ ounces (about 1 cup)	16
White	3⅓ ounces (about 1 cup)	13
Carrots	2 ounces (about 1 medium)	14
Cauliflower	3⅛ ounces (about 1 cup florets)	25
Celery	1 ounce (about 1 small stick)	2
Chile Pepper	⅓ ounce (about ¼ medium)	3
Corn kernels	2 ounces (about ⅓ cup)	14
Corn on the Cob (weighed whole)	7 ounces (1 ear)	123
Cucumber	1 ounce (about ¼ sliced)	2
Eggplant (broiled)	3½ ounces (about ¼ small)	75
Fennel	3½ ounces (about 1 cup sliced)	11
Leeks	2⅔ ounces (about 1 small)	16
Lettuce	2¾ ounces (about 1⅓ cups shredded)	13
Mushrooms	2¾ ounces (about 1 cup sliced)	10
Onions	5¼ ounces (about 1 large)	54
Parsnips	2¼ ounces (about ½ medium)	43
Peas	2½ ounces (about ½ cup)	55
Potatoes		
New (boiled)	6 ounces (about 3 medium)	116
Old (baked)	6 ounces (about 1 large)	245
Old (boiled)	6 ounces (about 1 medium)	126
Old (mashed with butter)	4¼ ounces (about 1 medium)	122
Old (roasted)	4½ ounces (about 1 medium)	151
Radishes	1¾ ounces (about ⅓ cup sliced)	6
Rutabaga	2 ounces (about ⅓ cup diced)	7
Scallions	⅓ ounce (about 2 small)	2
Spinach	3⅛ ounces (about 3 cups)	23
Squash (baked)	2¼ ounces (about ½ cup)	21
Sweet Potato (baked)	4½ ounces (about 1 small)	150
Tomatoes	3 ounces (about 1 small)	14
Tomatoes (broiled)	3 ounces (about 1 small)	42
Tomatoes, Cherry	3⅛ ounces (about 5 medium)	16
Zucchini	3⅛ ounces (about 1 small)	17

CHEESE

	Average portion	Calories
American, low-fat	1½ ounces	76
American, regular	1½ ounces	158
Brie	1½ ounces	144
Camembert	1½ ounces	116
Cheddar	1½ ounces	166
Cheese Spread	1 ounce	81
Cream Cheese, light	1 ounce	47
Cream Cheese, medium fat	1 ounce	74
Cottage, 4% fat	1½ ounces	36
Cottage, 2% fat	1½ ounces	28

	Average portion	Calories
Danish Blue	1 ounce	103
Dolcelatte	1½ ounces	158
Edam	1½ ounces	136
Emmental	1½ ounces	160
Feta	1¾ ounces	125
Gouda	1½ ounces	151
Monterey	1½ ounces	156
Mozzarella, fresh	2 ounces	141
Mozzarella, grated	2 ounces	164
Muenster	1½ ounces	155
Paneer	1½ ounces	130
Parmesan, freshly grated	¾ ounce	82
Ricotta	2 ounces	79
Roquefort	1 ounce	105
Stilton	1¼ ounces	143
EGGS		
Boiled	1¾ ounces (1 egg)	74
Fried	2 ounces (1 egg)	107
Poached	1¾ ounces (1 egg)	74
Omelet, Cheese	5¼ ounces (2 eggs)	399
Omelet, Plain	4¼ ounces (2 eggs)	180
Omelet, Spanish	5⅓ ounces (2 eggs)	229
Scrambled, no milk	3½ ounces (2 eggs)	160
Scrambled, with milk	4¼ ounces (2 eggs)	296
DAIRY		
Crème fraîche	1¾ ounces (about ¼ cup)	190
Crème fraîche, low fat	1¾ ounces (about ¼ cup)	85
Fromage blanc, plain	3½ ounces (about ⅓ cup)	113
Greek Yogurt, nonfat	3½ ounces (about ⅓ cup)	57
Milk		
Goat Milk	5 fluid ounces (about ⅓ cup)	88
Low-Fat Milk	5 fluid ounces (about ⅓ cup)	67
Skim Milk	5 fluid ounces (about ⅓ cup)	48
Soy Milk	5 fluid ounces (about ⅓ cup)	47
Whole Milk	5 fluid ounces (about ⅓ cup)	96
Sour Cream, Fat-Free	1 ounce (about 2 tablespoons)	29
Yogurt, plain nonfat	3½ ounces (about ⅓ cup)	46
MEAT		
Beef		
Braising Steak (braised)	5 ounces	315
Braising Steak (slow-cooked)	5 ounces	276
Ground, extra lean (stewed)	5 ounces	248
Tenderloin Steak (broiled)	5¾ ounces	316
Top Sirloin Steak (broiled)	5¾ ounces	287
Top Sirloin Steak strips (stir-fried)	3½ ounces	214
Tenderloin Steak (broiled)	5¾ ounces	292
Lamb		
Ground (stewed)	3⅛ ounces	187
Leg Cutlets (broiled)	3⅛ ounces	178
Loin Chops (broiled)	2½ ounces	149
Rack of Lamb (roasted)	3⅛ ounces	203
Shoulder Joint (roasted)	3⅛ ounces	212
Stewing (stewed)	4½ ounces	312
Organ Meats		
Liver, Lamb (fried)	3½ ounces	237
Liver, Ox (stewed)	2½ ounces	139
Liver, Pig (stewed)	2½ ounces	132
Livers, Chicken (fried)	2½ ounces	118

	Average portion	Calories
Pork, Bacon, and Ham		
Bacon		
Collar Joint (boiled)	1²/₃ ounce	88
Loin cutlets (broiled)	3½ ounces	191
Slices (dry-fried)	3½ ounces	295
Slices (broiled)	3½ ounces	214
Slices, dry-cured (broiled)	3½ ounces	257
Slices, smoked (broiled)	3½ ounces	293
Slices, sweet cure (broiled)	3½ ounces	258
Slices, Middle (broiled)	3½ ounces	307
Ground (stewed)	3⅛ ounces	172
Ham		
Ham, prosciutto	1²/₃ ounce	105
Ham, premium	2 ounces	74
Pork Shoulder, cured	3½ ounces	103
Leg Joint (roasted)	3⅛ ounces	164
Loin Chops (broiled)	2²/₃ ounces	140
Loin Cutlets (fried)	4¼ ounces	229
Loin Joint (pot-roasted)	3⅛ ounces	177
Pork, diced (stewed)	3⅛ ounces	166
Pork Cutlets (broiled)	4¾ ounces	228
Sparerib (broiled)	3¾ ounces	321
Sparerib (pot-roasted)	3⅛ ounces	181
Tenderloin of Pork (grilled)	4¼ ounces	240

POULTRY AND GAME

	Average portion	Calories
Chicken		
Breast, skinless (broiled)	4½ ounces	192
Breast strips (stir-fried)	3⅛ ounces	145
Drumsticks, skinned (casseroled)	1²/₃ ounces	87
Drumsticks, skinned (roasted)	1²/₃ ounces	71
Leg Quarter (roasted)	5 ounces	345
Leg Quarter, skinned (casseroled)	5 ounces	257
Thighs, skinless, boneless (casseroled)	1²/₃ ounces	81
Wings (broiled)	3½ ounces	274
Duck (roasted)	6½ ounces	361
Pheasant (roasted)	5²/₃ ounces	352
Pigeon (roasted)	4 ounces	215
Rabbit (stewed)	5²/₃ ounces	182
Turkey		
Breast, skinless (broiled)	3⅛ ounces	140
Drumsticks, skinned (roasted)	3⅛ ounces	146
Mince (stewed)	3⅛ ounces	158
Strips (stir-fried)	3⅛ ounces	148
Thighs, diced skinless, boneless (casseroled)	3⅛ ounces	163
Venison (roasted)	4¼ ounces	198

FISH AND SEAFOOD

	Average portion	Calories
Anchovies, in oil	⅓ ounce	28
Cod (baked)	4¼ ounces	115
Cod (poached)	4¼ ounces	113
Cod (steamed)	4¼ ounces	100
Cod, Smoked (poached)	4¼ ounces	121
Crab (boiled, dressed in shell)	4½ ounces	166
Crab, canned	1½ ounces	31
Flounder (broiled)	4½ ounces	125
Haddock (broiled)	4¼ ounces	125
Haddock (poached)	4¼ ounces	136
Haddock (steamed)	4¼ ounces	107
Haddock, Smoked (poached)	5⅓ ounces	201
Hake (broiled)	3½ ounces	113
Halibut (broiled)	5 ounces	175
Halibut (poached)	3¾ ounces	169

	Average portion	Calories
Halibut (steamed)	3¾ ounces	144
Kipper (baked)	4½ ounces	267
Kipper (broiled)	4½ ounces	332
Lobster (boiled, dressed in shell)	8¾ ounces	258
Mackerel (broiled)	5 ounces	351
Monkfish (broiled)	2½ ounces	67
Mussels (boiled, shelled)	1½ ounces	42
Red Snapper	3 ounces	85
Salmon (broiled)	3 ounces	176
Salmon (steamed)	2¾ ounces	152
Salmon, Smoked	2 ounces	80
Sardines (broiled)	1½ ounces	78
Scallops (steamed, shelled)	2½ ounces	83
Shrimp (boiled, shelled)	2 ounces	59
Swordfish (broiled)	4½ ounces	174
Trout, Brown (steamed)	5½ ounces	209
Trout, Rainbow (steamed)	5½ ounces	209
Tuna, canned	1⅔ ounces	45
Tuna, raw	1⅔ ounces	61

RICE, PASTA, AND BEANS (UNCOOKED, UNLESS OTHERWISE STATED)

Bulgur Wheat	3½ ounces (about ¾ cup)	338
Cannellini Beans, canned	3½ ounces (about ½ cup)	87
Chickpeas, canned	3½ ounces (about ½ cup)	115
Chickpeas, dried (boiled)	3½ ounces (about ⅔ cup)	121
Couscous	3½ ounces (about ½ cup)	364
Lentils, Green, canned	3½ ounces (about ½ cup)	118
Lentils, Green, dried (boiled)	3½ ounces (about ½ cup)	105
Lima Beans, canned	3½ ounces (about ⅓ cup)	77
Kidney Beans, canned	3½ ounces (about ⅓ cup)	100
Macaroni (boiled)	4½ ounces (about 1 cup)	108
Noodles, Egg (boiled)	4½ ounces (about ¾ cup)	78
Noodles (fried)	4½ ounces (about ¾ cup)	191
Rice		
Brown (boiled)	4½ ounces (about ⅔ cup)	176
White, glutinous (boiled)	4½ ounces (about ¾ cup)	82
White, regular (boiled)	4½ ounces (about ¾ cup)	154
Spaghetti (boiled)	4½ ounces (about 1 cup)	130
Spaghetti, whole-wheat (boiled)	4½ ounces (about 1 cup)	141

BREAD

Ciabatta, plain	1¾ ounces (1 slice)	135
Croissants	2 ounces (1 medium)	224
French Bread	1½ ounces (1 small slice)	109
Garlic Bread	¾ ounce (1 small slice)	73
Hamburger/Hotdog Bun	1½ ounces (1 bun)	120
Hot Cross Buns	1¾ ounces (1 bun)	155
Italian bread	1 ounce (1 large slice)	81
Muffins, English, white	2 ounces (1 muffin)	134
Pita Bread, white	2 ounces (6½-inch diameter)	165
Rolls		
White, crusty	1¾ ounces (1 large roll)	131
White, soft	1⅔ ounces (2 dinner rolls)	114
Whole-Wheat	1⅔ ounces (2 dinner rolls)	117
Sliced		
Multigrain	1¼ ounces (about 1¼ slices)	92
Rye	1 ounce (about 1 slice)	83
White	1½ ounces (about 1½ slices)	94
Whole-Wheat	1½ ounces (about 1½ slices)	93
Soda Bread, Irish	4½ ounces (one thick slice)	267
Tortilla, soft	1¾ ounces (one 8-inch)	146

	Average portion	Calories
CEREALS		
Bran Flakes	1 ounce (about ¾ cup)	95
Cheerios	1 ounce (about 1 cup)	103
Corn Flakes	1 ounce (about 1 cup)	108
Frosted Flakes	1 ounce (about ¾ cup)	113
Muesli	1¾ ounces (about ⅔ cup)	184
Oat Flakes	1 ounce (about ¾ cup)	107
Oatmeal, with milk and water	5⅔ ounces (about ⅔ cup)	133
Oatmeal, with water	5⅔ ounces (about ⅔ cup)	78
Oatmeal, with whole milk	5⅔ ounces (about ⅔ cup)	186
Puffed Wheat	¾ ounce (about 1⅓ cups)	64
Raisin Bran	2 ounces (about 1 cup)	187
Rice Pops	1 ounce (about 1 cup)	111
Wheat, Shredded	1⅔ ounces (1 biscuit)	150
Wheat, Shredded, mini	1⅔ ounces (about 1 cup)	154
Whole-Wheat Biscuits	1⅓ ounces (about 2 biscuits)	134
JAMS AND SPREADS		
Honey	½ ounce (about 1 tablespoon)	91
Jam	½ ounce (about 2 teaspoons)	39
Lemon Curd	½ ounce (1 tablespoon)	42
Marmalade	½ ounce (about 2 teaspoons)	26
Peanut Butter, chunky	¾ ounce (about 1 tablespoon)	152
Peanut Butter, smooth	¾ ounce (about 1 tablespoon)	156
Yeast Extract	⅛ ounce (about 1 teaspoon)	9
DIPS		
Guacamole	1⅔ ounces (about 3 tablespoons)	58
Hummus	1 ounce (about 2 tablespoons)	56
COLD DRINKS AND JUICES		
Apple Juice	5⅔ ounces (about ⅔ cup)	61
Carrot Juice	5⅔ ounces (about ⅔ cup)	38
Cola	5⅔ ounces (about ⅔ cup)	66
Cola, diet	5⅔ ounces (about ⅔ cup)	Trace
Grapefruit Juice	5⅔ ounces (about ⅔ cup)	53
Lemon-Flavored Soda	5⅔ ounces (about ⅔ cup)	35
Lemon-Flavor Soda, diet	5⅔ ounces (about ⅔ cup)	Trace
Orange Juice, fresh	5⅔ ounces (about ⅔ cup)	53
Pineapple Juice	5⅔ ounces (about ⅔ cup)	66
Pomegranate Juice	5⅔ ounces (about ⅔ cup)	70
HOT DRINKS		
Cappuccino, with low-fat milk	6¾ ounces (about ¾ cup)	46
Coffee, with low-fat milk	6¾ ounces (about ¾ cup)	13
Coffee, with skim milk	6¾ ounces (about ¾ cup)	8
Coffee, with whole milk	6¾ ounces (about ¾ cup)	15
Hot Chocolate, with low-fat milk	6¾ ounces (about ¾ cup)	135
Hot Chocolate, with skim milk	6¾ ounces (about ¾ cup)	112
Hot Chocolate, with whole milk	6¾ ounces (about ¾ cup)	171
Latte, with low-fat milk	6¾ ounces (about ¾ cup)	60
Latte, with skim milk	6¾ ounces (about ¾ cup)	33
Latte, with whole milk	6¾ ounces (about ¾ cup)	85
Tea, black	6¾ ounces (about ¾ cup)	Trace
Tea, Chinese	6¾ ounces (about ¾ cup)	2
Tea, green	6¾ ounces (about ¾ cup)	Trace
Tea, herbal	6¾ ounces (about ¾ cup)	2
Tea, with low-fat milk	6¾ ounces (about ¾ cup)	13
Tea, with skim milk	6¾ ounces (about ¾ cup)	8
Tea, with whole milk	6¾ ounces (about ¾ cup)	15

Index

Acknowledgments

Publisher: Sarah Ford
Managing Editor: Clare Churly
Designer: Eoghan O'Brien
Layouts by Jeremy Tiltson
Senior Production Manager: Peter Hunt